CHARLES POWELL LESLIE (II)'S ESTATES AT GLASLOUGH, COUNTY MONAGHAN, 1800–41

Maynooth Studies in Irish Local History

SERIES EDITOR Raymond Gillespie

This is one of six new pamphlets in the Maynooth Studies in Irish Local History Series to be published in the year 2001 which brings the number published to forty. Like their predecessors most of the pamphlets are based on theses completed as part of the M.A. in local history programme in National University of Ireland, Maynooth. While the regions and time span which they cover are diverse, from Cork city to Tyrone, they all share a conviction that the exploration of the local past can shed light on the evolution of modern societies. They each demonstrate that understanding the evolution of local societies is important. The local worlds of Ireland in the past are as complex and sophisticated as the national framework in which they are set. The communities which peopled those local worlds, whether they be the inhabitants of large cities, housing on the edge of those cities or rural estates, shaped and were shaped by their environments to create a series of interlocking worlds of considerable complexity. Those past worlds are best interpreted not through local administrative divisions, such as the county, but in human units: local places where communities of people lived and died. Untangling what held these communities together, and what drove them apart, gives us new insights into the world we have lost.

These pamphlets each make a significant contribution to understanding Irish society in the past. Together with thirty-four earlier works in this series they explore something of the hopes and fears of those who lived in Irish local communities in the past. In doing so they provide examples of the practice of local history at its best and show the vibrant discipline which the study of local history in Ireland has become in recent years.

Maynooth Studies in Irish Local History: Number 38

Charles Powell Leslie (II)'s estates at Glaslough, County Monaghan, 1800–41

Portrait of a landed estate business and its community in changing times

Anthony Doyle

IRISH ACADEMIC PRESS
DUBLIN • PORTLAND, OR

First published in 2001 by
IRISH ACADEMIC PRESS
44, Northumberland Road, Dublin 4, Ireland
and in the United States of America by
IRISH ACADEMIC PRESS
c/o ISBS, 5824 NE Hassalo Street, Portland, OR 97213–3644.

website: www.iap.ie

British Library Cataloguing in Publication Data
Doyle, Anthony
Charles Powell Leslie (II)'s estates at Glaslough, County Monaghan, 1800–1841: portrait of a landed estate business and its community in changing times. – (Maynooth studies in Irish local history; no. 38)
1. Leslie, Charles Powell 2. Landowners – Ireland – Monaghan – Biography 3. Land use, Rural – Ireland – Monaghan – History – 19th century 4. Country life – Ireland – Monaghan – History – 19th century 5. Monaghan (Ireland) – Social conditions – 19th century
I. Title
941.6'97'081'092
ISBN 0–7165–2739–1

A catalog record of this book is avalable from the Library of Congress

Typeset in 10 pt on 12 pt Bembo by
Carrigboy Typesetting Services, County Cork
Printed by Creative Print and Design (Wales) Ebbw Vale

Contents

Preface

I wish to acknowledge with gratitude some of the many people who encouraged and supported me in completing this work. I am indebted to the Leslie family of Castle Leslie, Glaslough, especially Sir John Leslie (4th baronet) who first kindled my interest in the local history of north County Monaghan, also his niece Samantha who helped me with the family's private collection of papers; to Captain Gary Roberts, minister of Glaslough, who gave me access to the Church of Ireland records for the parish of Donagh; to Victor Buckley of the National Monuments & Historic Properties Service; to Dr Jackie Hill my supervisor for the M.A. in local history, for her guidance and support; to Dr Ray Gillespie, the programme co-ordinator for the M.A. in local history; my classmates in the M.A. in local history course at N.U.I. Maynooth for their enthusiasm for local history and companionship; to the staffs of the many libraries and repositories, especially T.C.D. library, the R.D.S. library, the R.C.B. library, National Library of Ireland, National Archives of Ireland, Public Record Office of Northern Ireland, Monaghan County Museum, Monaghan County Library and the Russell library and the John Paul II library, N.U.I. Maynooth, for their help and courtesy. Finally, I wish to thank my wife Helen, my parents and my family, for their patience, support and encouragement throughout this work.

I dedicate this study to my father Kevin Doyle (1925–2000).

Introduction

This pamphlet endeavours to reconstruct the world of the landlord and tenant in north County Monaghan before the Famine by focusing on the estates of the Leslie family at Glaslough. These estates were principally located in the civil parish of Donagh, which was co-extensive with the Catholic and Church of Ireland parishes of the same name in the early nineteenth century. The Leslies' estates covered a large area of this parish and their tenants made up a significant part of the local community. The study examines Charles Powell Leslie II's management of his estates, the effect of his management on the community's development, the impact of external events on the community, and the changes within this community and its rural economy in the years between the act of union and the 1840s famine.

Ireland experienced significant changes, both social and economical, during these years. The economy was buoyant during the Napoleonic war years prior to 1815, after which it declined never regaining its wartime levels before mid century. Living conditions deteriorated in line with the economic decline. In parallel with these changes, the relationship and attitudes of the Catholic and Protestant communities within Irish society changed considerably. In response to these changing times there was also a transformation in the attitudes of landlords to their estates and their tenants. Kerby Miller in his study *Emigrants and exiles* (1985) described the general response of landlords to the economic changes:[1]

> After 1814, changes of ownership and economic necessities accelerated the transformation of a paternalistic or negligent gentry into a class of landed businessmen ... efficiency and profits now took precedence over archaic ideals of honor and noblesse oblige. One result was a sharp reduction of investments in beautification projects, local industries, and public works which had formerly provided employment to artisans and labourers. Another was the elimination of middlemen, ... [Landlords assumed] greater control over their properties in an effort to extract larger, more punctually paid incomes ... [They modernised] farming methods on their estates ... [and] in order to gain increased control over their tenants, proprietors accelerated the trend toward shorter leases begun in the eighteenth century.

Landlords were key figures in the economic, social and political life of pre-famine rural Ireland. W.A. Maguire's study *The Downshire estates in Ireland*,

1801–1845 (1972) illustrated the value of analysing landed estates to shed more light on the structure of society in rural Ireland before the Famine. He regarded estate records as 'the most untapped source of information available to historians'.[2] James S. Donnelly echoes these views in his comprehensive study *The land and the people of nineteenth-century Cork* (1975) commenting that estate records 'have been surprisingly little used for studies concerned with the agrarian economy and the land question.'[3] By analysing these sources, stereotypical views of landlords can be stripped away to reveal what landlords did as distinct from what they were alleged to have done. The famine of the 1840s was a disaster for rural communities and as Maguire comments, 'made such an impression upon contemporary opinion, that the half-century which preceded it tended to be viewed as the menacing prelude to 1845 rather than as a historical period deserving study for its own sake.'[4] Both government and public opinion viewed the landlord and the landed estate system as the obvious scapegoat for the 1840s disaster. The concept of the alien landlord preying mercilessly on the people once established was accepted as the rule. This view was echoed by Freeman in his study *Pre-famine Ireland* (1957) commenting: 'Although some of the landlords tried to improve the life of the neighbourhood, as a class they were already discredited, alienated from the people in outlook and generally in religion, and held largely responsible for the woes of multitudes.'[5] However, the problem with generalisation and treating Ireland as a unit when discussing its social history are known. In many ways rural Ireland in the early nineteenth century was a collection of island estate communities rather than a homogenous nation. Thus when discussing how landlords managed their estates and how the communities living on them changed over time, each estate and its community is worthwhile to examine, as each had its own distinctiveness. Further, by studying different estates we can broaden our understanding of Irish social history and help remove the veil of preconception and generalisation.

There have been a number of historical studies written on County Monaghan, some specifically referring to the parish of Donagh and the Leslies of Glaslough. Of these some focus on the concept of family history with an emphasis on genealogy, in particular, E.P. Shirley's *The history of the County of Monaghan* (1879) and Seymour Leslie's *Glaslough in the kingdom of Oriel and noted men who have dwelt there* (1913).[6] Others, like Peadar Livingstone's *The Monaghan story* (1980), described developments in a county context and discuss them in terms of national events.[7] Patrick Duffy has carried out a number of studies on the change in the rural landscape, land ownership and society in County Monaghan. In particular he has analysed the southern County Monaghan estate of the Shirley family in the mid-nineteenth century.[8] None of these studies have carried out a microscopic analysis of the social and economic developments on north County Monaghan estates in the years between the act of union and the 1840s famine. This study, by examining the

Leslie estates during these years, endeavours to fill this gap. Further, existing studies do not appear to have used the rich primary source material in the private collection of papers in the Leslie family archives at Castle Leslie. In carrying out this study the author has used this source material and hopes his analysis of this material adds to the body of knowledge and understanding of landlords, their landed estates and associated communities between 1800 and 1841, with particular reference to north County Monaghan. Landed estates in north County Monaghan differed from estates in south Monaghan in that the community had more in common with their neighbours in Counties Armagh and Tyrone than their southern counterparts, who lived close to the Leinster counties of Louth and Meath. Further, the parish of Donagh had a significant Protestant community, many of whom were members of the Church of Ireland and thus shared similar religious views and outlook as their landlords, the Leslies. This gave the estate another attribute, which made it different to the majority of landed estates in Ireland where the landlord and tenant were divided by their religion.

Charles Powell Leslie II came to national attention on a number of occasions, most notably as the opponent whom the Catholic Association defeated in the 1826 County Monaghan election and as colonel of the Monaghan militia, which was engaged in suppressing the 1798 rebellion in Counties Down and Antrim. In 1826, Daniel O'Connell described him as 'one of the most uncompromising enemies of his Catholic countrymen'.[9] Brendan O'Grady in his study of the migrants to Prince Edward Island, Canada, some of whom were from Leslie's estates, quotes a description of Leslie, 'although having the reputation of a good landlord had agents and sub-agents who were hard and cruel.'[10] These views will be explored in this pamphlet in the context of Leslie's estate management and his relationship and interaction with the community living on his estates. The analysis of Charles Powell Leslie II's military and political career is, however, beyond the scope of this essay. The reader interested in these topics is referred to: Martin Cahill's essay in the *Clogher Record*, 'The 1826 general election in County Monaghan' for a description of Leslie's role in this election; Christopher McGimpsey's thesis on County Monaghan elections between 1800 and 1868 for the politics in County Monaghan in the early nineteenth century; and, one of the many histories of the 1798 rebellion in Counties Down and Antrim such as, A.T.Q. Stewart's *The summer soldiers: The 1798 rebellion in Antrim and Down* for Leslie's involvement in the suppression of the 1798 rebellion.[11]

The main primary source for this study is the Leslie papers. These papers are held partly in the private collection of the Leslie family at Castle Leslie, Glaslough, and partly in the National Library of Ireland.[12] These papers include correspondence, rent rolls, accounts and management documentation related to the estates at Glaslough for the period 1800 to 1841. Other important primary sources related to the local community under study are the church records. The baptisms, marriage, burials and vestry records of the Church of Ireland parish of Donagh are complete between 1800 and 1841. The majority of these records are held in local custody in the parish's archive in the church at Glaslough, County Monaghan. The Public Record Office of Northern Ireland have microfilm copies also which include some items no longer in local custody. The records of the Presbyterian congregation at Glennan in the parish of Donagh, though less comprehensive, commence in 1805, and are on microfilm in the Public Record Office of Northern Ireland. Unfortunately, the parish's Catholic registers for this period are generally illegible. A wide variety of other primary sources have been used to support these sources and reveal different aspects of the Leslies' estates and the community living on them. These sources include parliamentary papers, private correspondence, ordnance survey memoirs and maps, and contemporary publications such as Samuel Lewis' *A topographical dictionary of Ireland* and Coote's *Statistical survey of the county of Monaghan with observations on the means of improvement.*[13]

The first chapter of this study describes the Leslie family, their politics, careers, and their links with the community living on their north County Monaghan estates. This chapter also describes the parish of Donagh: its communities, its agriculture and industries, its population's way of life and the changes in its society between 1800 and 1841, creating a picture of life in Donagh during these years. The second chapter describes Charles Powell Leslie II's management of his estates at Glaslough. This chapter explores the relationship between the Leslies and their agents, examines the performance of the Leslie estates as a business and discusses Charles Powell Leslie II's politics in the context of this business. The third chapter explores the changes in the local community living on the estates in the years between 1800 and 1841. In particular this chapter examines the impact of the post 1815 recession on this community, the Leslies' response to this recession and the decline in living conditions within the parish of Donagh.

The Leslies of Glaslough and the parish of Donagh

The Leslies' home has been in Glaslough, County Monaghan, since 1665 when John Leslie, bishop of Clogher, settled there. The district had been part of the MacMahon territory until 1608, when it was confiscated and granted to Sir Thomas Ridgeway, who built Glaslough Castle, a square tower, around which the house was subsequently built.[1] In 1661, Bishop John Leslie was awarded £2,000 pounds sterling by the house of commons as a reward for his support of King Charles II.[2] Shortly after receipt of this gift, in his ninty-fifth year, he bought the Glaslough estate from the Ridgeway Trustees.[3]

Bishop John Leslie married Katherine Conyngham in 1638 and their eldest surviving son, Dean John Leslie, inherited his father's estate in 1671 when the bishop died.[4] The bishop's younger surviving son, Charles Leslie, the non-juror, a zealous opponent of Catholicism and King James II's reforms, could not reconcile his conscience to take the oath of allegiance to King William and Queen Mary following the glorious revolution in 1688.[5] So he followed the exiled royal family abroad. The closeness of Charles Leslie and his son Robert to the Stuart cause, during these years, endangered family members and threatened the Leslies' estates in Ireland. In March 1718, Charles Leslie wrote to the duke of Mar 'I have ill news that a lawsuit is commenced in Ireland against the only fortune I have left to give bread to my family there and I have none there to defend it.'[6] A letter from James III, the Stuart king in exile, to Lieutenant-general Dillon, in May 1718, refers to a project, for which Robert Leslie requested the king's support.[7] Dean John's wife, Elizabeth, writing to Robert, her husband's heir, inviting him to visit the County Monaghan estates in 1720, advised he should use 'discreet caution' in such a visit.[8] These links to the Stuart cause continued to haunt the family in the nineteenth century. During the 1826 County Monaghan election, Charles Powell Leslie II had to defend his and the Leslies' loyalty to the Protestant cause from his opponents' attacks, which referred to his ancestors' support of the Stuarts.[9]

Dean John Leslie died in 1721 and his younger brother Charles Leslie died the following year, 1722.[10] Charles' son Robert inherited the lands around Glaslough. Robert Leslie appears to have had financial difficulties in the early eighteenth century. In 1735, he made an application to parliament, so that he could sell parts of the estates at Glaslough and Emy, in order to pay 'debts and incumbrances affecting the said lands, and of other debts of Robert Leslie.'[11]

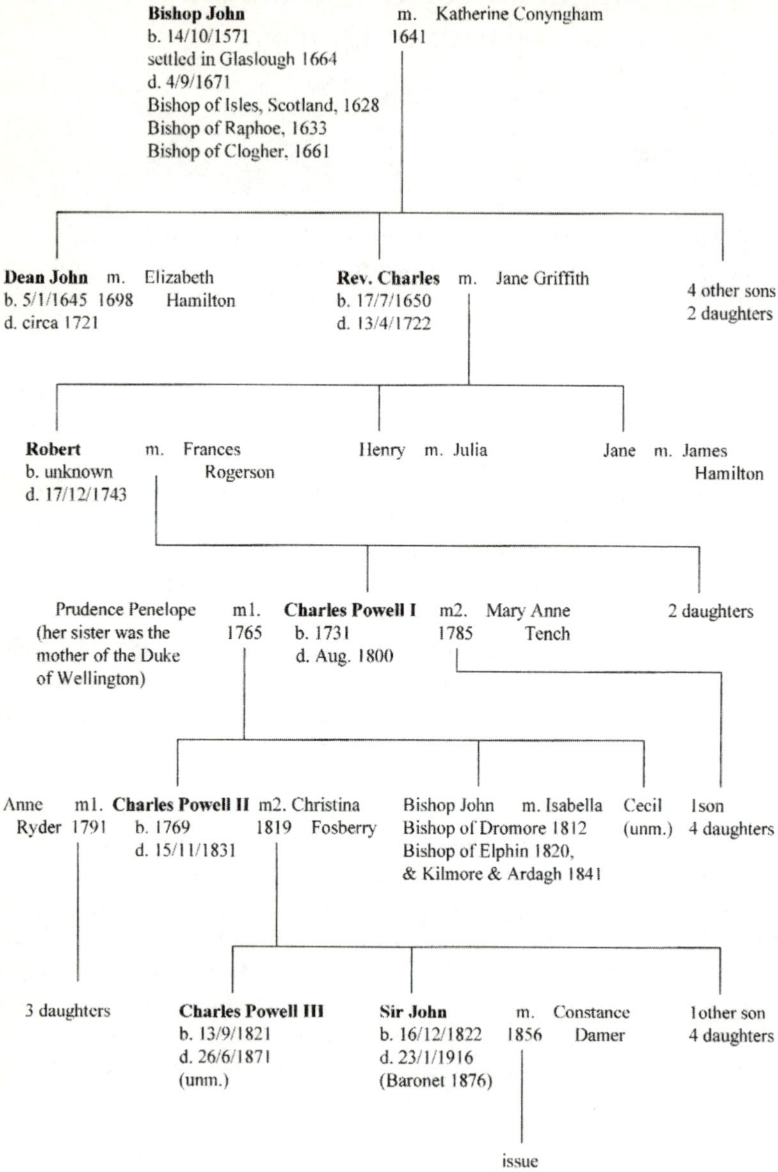

1. Leslies' of Castle Leslie family tree

In the following year, 1736, a number of townlands were advertised for sale.[12] However, Robert Leslie does not appear to have been actively interested in the estates.[13] In 1743, he died while his son and heir, Charles Powell Leslie I, was still a minor. The financial and political difficulties, which the Leslie family experienced in the first half of the eighteenth century no doubt affected the attitudes and perspectives of both Charles Powell Leslie I and his son Charles Powell Leslie II.

Unlike his father, Charles Powell Leslie I was interested in the development of his estates. Arthur Young, who visited the Leslie estate in 1776 during his tour of Ireland, noted Leslie as an improving landlord who had a good understanding of the business of his estate, active in its management, and was committed to its development.[14] His improvements coupled with the economic boom in the second half of the eighteenth century provided the Leslies with significant increased rental income. In 1752 the Glaslough and Emy estates returned a combined annual rental income of £953 (at this time the Emyvale estate was referred to as the Emy estate).[15] This was similar to the £1,000 that Elizabeth Leslie, Robert Leslie's aunt, thought the two estates could give him in 1720.[16] The 1760s were years of rapid growth. The rental income on the Glaslough and Emyvale estates rose from £1,072 in 1761 to £1,979 in 1766.[17] In subsequent years the growth was only marginal. By 1799 the combined annual income from the two estates was £2,140.[18]

Charles Powell Leslie I was also active in politics. He served as sheriff for County Monaghan in 1761.[19] He was the colonel of the Monaghan volunteers of the late eighteenth century. In 1771, he was the first member of the Leslie family to become an M.P. (Member of Parliament), representing Hillsborough, County Down.[20] In 1783 he was elected M.P. for County Monaghan and continued to represent the county until his death in 1800.[21] As an M.P. Charles Powell Leslie I was noted as anti-government and part of the patriot party throughout this period. He consistently opposed the Act of Union until his death in 1800. His politics were to maintain the power of the ascendancy class to which he belonged. Thus believing that the Act of Union undermined that power he opposed it. When he died, Charles Powell Leslie I's family's position and his estates, were much improved compared with when he came into his inheritance. There was a prosperous socially developed community living on the estates at Glaslough. From his two marriages he had eight children. His eldest son from his first marriage, Colonel Charles Powell Leslie II, succeeded to his estates, the most significant being those at Glaslough and at Pettigo in County Donegal.

Charles Powell Leslie II was born circa 1769 and was educated at Christchurch, Oxford.[22] In October 1791 he married Anne Ryder and through this marriage he came into possession of an estate in Leicestershire.[23] They had three daughters. Anne died in 1813 and Leslie married Christina Fosberry in 1819.[24] From this marriage they had seven children, including Leslie's successor

2. Charles Powell Leslie II (1769–1831)

Charles Powell Leslie III, and John Leslie who succeeded his childless elder brother in 1871 and was knighted in 1876.[25] Charles Powell Leslie II served as a sheriff of County Monaghan in 1788–9.[26] He was appointed colonel of the Monaghan regiment of militia in 1797, a post he held until his death in 1831.[27] Although he failed initially to succeed his father as M.P. for County Monaghan, he won the seat unopposed in 1801, when his rival Warner William Westenra succeeded to the peerage, as Lord Rossmore.[28] In 1803 Leslie was appointed governor of County Monaghan.[29] His participation in parliament required that he live in London during parliamentary sessions, so that he was resident in Glaslough for only part of the year, managing his estates through his agents. In Thorne's *The history of parliament, the house of commons, 1790–1820*, Leslie was described as 'a cunning fox and a deep politician' by a contemporary.[30] Throughout his parliamentary career he generally supported the government, particularly, when his relatives the Wellesley and Ryder brothers were part of the administration, however, he consistently opposed Catholic relief bills, which contributed towards the loss of his seat in the 1826 election.[31]

In the early nineteenth century, County Monaghan returned two M.P.s to parliament. Prior to 1826 there had been no contested election in the county since the Act of Union. The two seats were shared between the Protestant gentry of the county. The concepts of party, which we are familiar with today was not developed. Brian Walker in his work *Parliamentary election results in*

Ireland, 1801–1922, makes no attempt to classify candidates before 1832 as party allegiance was ill defined.[32] Therefore these Monaghan gentry politicians had allegiance to their own and their friends goals and ambitions rather than to a party philosophy. Charles Powell Leslie II represented one of the county's political groups, while the Dawson family led the other. In the eighteenth century the Rossmore/Westenra family had represented the borough of Monaghan. This borough ceased to return an M.P. following the Act of Union. Thus throughout the early nineteenth century, this family endeavoured to establish their political position in County Monaghan exploiting different alliances to do so.[33] However, they had to wait until 1818, when Dawson became a peer, before Henry Robert Westenra, Rossmore's son, was returned as M.P for the county. The entry of Evelyn John Shirley into the political arena in the 1820s meant that either Leslie or Westenra would be unseated, as Shirley with his large estate in south County Monaghan had successfully registered a large number of his Catholic tenants to vote in time for the 1826 election.[34] Both the Rossmore and Dawson families supported Catholic claims uniting them against Charles Powell Leslie II who opposed these claims. The alliance of the Rossmore and Dawson families, exploiting the Catholic Association's influence, gave the victory to Westenra at Leslie's expense. In 1830, the year before he died, Charles Powell Leslie II became M.P. for the borough of New Ross, avoiding an expensive election contest for a County Monaghan seat, while regaining his M.P.'s influence.[35]

Charles Powell Leslie II's Glaslough estates were primarily located in the parish of Donagh in north County Monaghan (figure 3). This parish was and still is situated on the roads from Monaghan to Belfast and Dublin to Derry. Its main settlements were the town of Glaslough and the village of Emyvale. The Ordnance Survey memoirs of the 1830s recorded its extreme length as nine miles and its extreme breadth as six and a half miles, containing over 16,202 acres.[36] Donagh is located on the limestone lowland corridor extending south-westward from north Armagh into Monaghan, continuing to the upper Erne. It is covered with small drumlins and is one of the most favoured areas in County Monaghan.[37] The Blackwater and its tributary, the Mountain Water, drain the land and it has a number of lakes including one at Glaslough.

At the beginning of the nineteenth century there were demesnes at Glaslough, Anketell's Grove and Falkland in this parish. Between Glaslough and Falkland there were immense tracts of bog.[38] The parish of Donagh and its neighbour, Errigal Trough, together formed the barony of Trough, which was divided primarily between the Leslie, Anketell and Singleton families, with holdings in more homogenous blocks than in some parts of Ireland. This homogenity and the presence of resident landlords like the Leslies had a significant influence on the settlement in this area. It facilitated more effective colonisation of the parish of Donagh by Protestant settlers, as there was greater consistency of policy in the community's development. The original

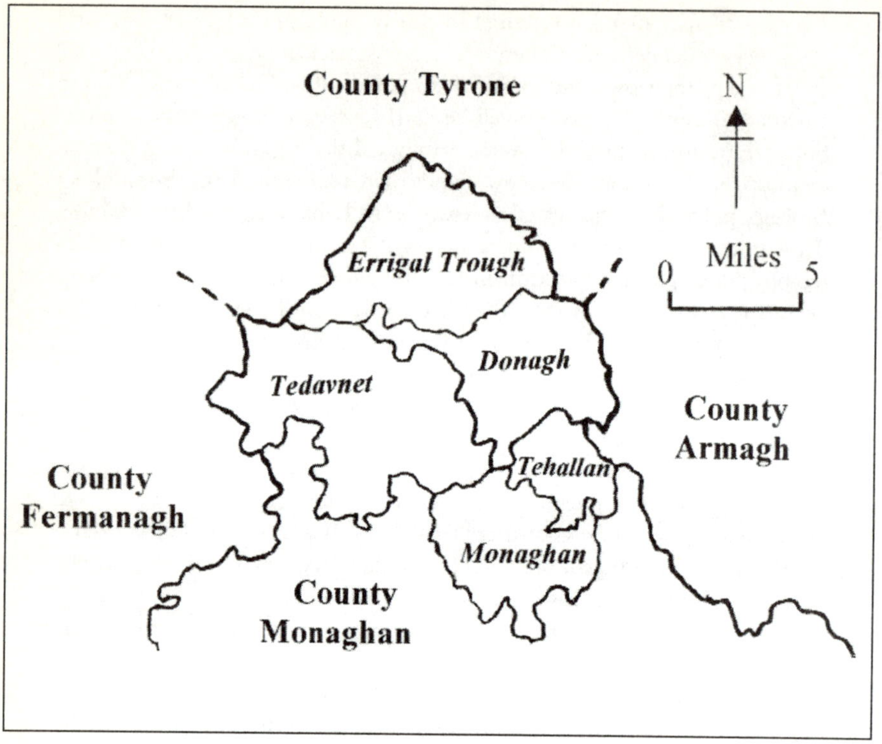

3. Civil parish of Donagh, County Monaghan

parish centre was around the medieval church in the townland of Donagh. In 1670 the Church of Ireland community transferred the church to Glaslough and this was later re-built in 1763.[39] The village of Glaslough had developed near the Ridgeway castle in the seventeenth century. In the poll money return of 1660, which only recorded heads of families, it had the highest population concentration in the parish with forty-one people (families), twenty-four whom were English and the remaining seventeen Irish.[40] The neighbouring village of Emyvale, then known as Skernageeragh, was a small settlement with ten people (families), six English and four Irish.[41] During the eighteenth century Donagh's population grew. A significant proportion of this population was Protestant of both Church of Ireland and Presbyterian denominations, the latter congregation had worshipped in the parish from the seventeenth century.[42] The 1766 religious census, although of questionable accuracy, gives a sense of the ratio of Protestant to Catholic for Donagh in comparison with its neighbouring parishes, see table 1.

Table 1. 1766 religious census in north County Monaghan

Parish	Families		
	Protestant	Papist	Priests
Errigal Trough	120	700	2
Donagh	408	576	1
Monaghan	479	721	2
Tedavnet	258	264	2
Tehallan	96	315	–

Source: Religious Census 1766: Diocese of Clogher, summary for diocese, Return No. 703 (N.A.I., M.2476 (d)).

In the early nineteenth century this ratio of Protestants to Catholics living in Donagh was practically unchanged from the 1766 census, see table 2.

Table 2. Civil population by religious denomination, 1831

Civil Parish	Roman Catholic		Church of Ireland		Presbyterian	
	Population	*Percentage of total*	*Population*	*Percentage of total*	*Population*	*Percentage of total*
Donagh	6,696	60	1,950	18	2,422	22

Source: *First report of the commissioners of public instruction, Ireland*, p. 12a, H.C. 1835, xxxiii.

Throughout the period under study while those of Catholic faith were the largest community in the parish, the Presbyterian and Church of Ireland communities were significant. However, despite their majority, the Catholic community had no political weight in early nineteenth century Monaghan. Wakefield writing on Monaghan, at this time, noted that although the majority of the population were Catholic, the county was controlled by the Protestant landowners.[43] There were no Catholic estates in the county, nor Catholics on the grand jury or as officers in the Monaghan militia.[44]

This Protestant dominance also existed at local level where the parish's civil administration in the eighteenth and early nineteenth centuries was managed to a large part through the vestry meetings of the Church of Ireland community. The parish vestry records and registers provide evidence of this community's civic spirit and loyalty to maintaining a Hanoverian British Protestant way of life. This is clearly seen by the peek in the number of marriages in 1803. The three months with the highest number of marriages over the forty-year period occurred in 1803. The registers recorded four marriages in each of the months of May and July and seven marriages in the month of June.[45] The probable explanation for this desire among the parishioners to get married can be found many miles from north County Monaghan, in the corridors of government in London and Paris. On the 16 May 1803, war was renewed between Napoleonic France and Britain. The bridegrooms in three of the four marriages between 25 May and 30 May were members of the Monaghan regiment of militia, while the bridegrooms in nine of the eleven marriages in the following two months were also in the militia. The commencement of this war stimulated national fervour and pride. In the midst of this excitement, men and women thought of their future. Men enlisted in the military, their parents and neighbours were proud of their patriotism, and they looked resplendent in their uniforms when compared to their civilian clothes. The registers record these emotions and attitudes of loyalty amongst the parishioners in Donagh, reflecting global events at a local level. The Church of Ireland vestry minutes also reflect this national fervour recording the raising of troops for the militia, which acted as part of the army of reserve. Recruiting sergeants were appointed and funds raised by the parish in August 1803, October 1807 and April 1810.[46] This national pride amongst this community was again demonstrated in February 1820, following the death of King George III, when 'The church was hung in black . . . at the expense of the parish'.[47] The Presbyterian community also demonstrated this loyalty to king and country. The Presbyterian registers record the importance to this community of serving the nation. Fourteen of the bridegrooms in the marriages between 1805 and 1820 were in the Monaghan militia and six other bridegrooms were serving in the regular army.[48]

Many Protestants had settled in Donagh with the growth in the linen industry in the eighteenth century. At the beginning of the nineteenth-century the parish of Donagh was typical of the proto-industrialised economic, social and settlement pattern which had developed in eighteenth-century Ulster. Coote described the agriculture and industry in the area in 1801.[49] He commented that the crops grown were mainly potatoes and oats and that 'scarcely a cabin is without a loom or two' as linen manufacture was increasing and their chief dependence. Their webs were sold in the Armagh and Monaghan markets. Contiguous to the town of Glaslough there was a good brewery, which supplied the neighbourhood. The area had excellent potter's clay and there was a pottery in the townland of Lisgoa. Over a hundred carpenters resided near Glennan who were constantly employed in manufacturing furnishings for sale at the neighbouring fairs and markets, exploiting the availability of cheap timber from the neighbourhood woods such as the hundred acre ash wood at Glaslough.[50] The parish had some quarries including a grey marble quarry at Glennan, which employed twenty people and a quarry of green stone which was located in the bed of a river flowing through the Anketell demesne.[51] These quarries continued to be important in the parish economy throughout the early nineteenth century, Lewis remarking on their output in 1837.[52] There were a number of mills associated with the agriculture and local industries of the parish. Coote's description of Robert McMorran's mill, which worked iron, located at Emyvale illustrates the operation of one such mill:[53]

> principally spades, shovels, and heavy work, which are forged by the sledge, worked with water ... In this forge sixty spades will be finished in one day by the work of three men; one to the bellows, one to the fire, and a third to hold the bar under the sledge, which is raised by a low crank from the water-wheel, fifteen inches above the anvil, and strikes twenty-four blows in a minute.

Mills like this continued in operation throughout the early-nineteenth century as part of the local agricultural economy. The Ordnance survey memoirs recorded seven mills in the parish of Donagh in 1838.[54] Four of these were on the Leslie estates. The size of these mills and their function varied. William Young's corn and flax mills employed about twenty people.[55] Bernard McCanagh's mill in Aghnagap was a stone house with a thatched roof and its wheel drove only a single pair of stones.[56] William Murdock's mill in Emyvale was in a good stone house with a slated roof and its wheel drove two-pair of stones, one lifting machine, two sets of fans, two screens and four sets of elevators.[57] John Collins' mill in Drumully had one-set of scutches and one-set of rollers.[58] The mills had different capabilities depending on the rural industry which they were associated with, some had stones for corn, others scutches for flax. In 1837, Lewis remarked in his topographical dictionary that an extensive flour-mill had been built recently near Glaslough, obtaining its wheat supply at the Glaslough market.[59] He also commented that 'the linen manufacture is carried on to a considerable extent' in the parish of Donagh.[60] He noted that mills were being built for scutching and spinning flax, and that a factory was being built on a large scale for weaving linens by hand and power looms, which when completed would employ between eight and nine hundred people. Thus although the linen industry had changed since the eighteenth-century, the presence of flax and scutching mills, coupled with Lewis's remarks indicates that the linen industry was still important in the local economy in the 1830s.

The town of Glaslough and Emyvale village were the most significant settlements in the parish of Donagh. A lease between Charles Powell Leslie I and William Ogle for Emyvale may have stimulated the growth of this settlement.[61] Prior to this lease of 1767 Emyvale is referred to as Skernageeragh in the estate rent rolls.[62] In the mid-eighteenth century this settlement appears to have been small, as the estate papers record only eight houses in the 'town of Skernageeragh' as compared to Glaslough's seventy houses in 1763.[63] In 1801, Coote described Emyvale as 'a neat and clean, though poor village with very little trade, and has no market: around, it is inhabited by weavers.'[64] The

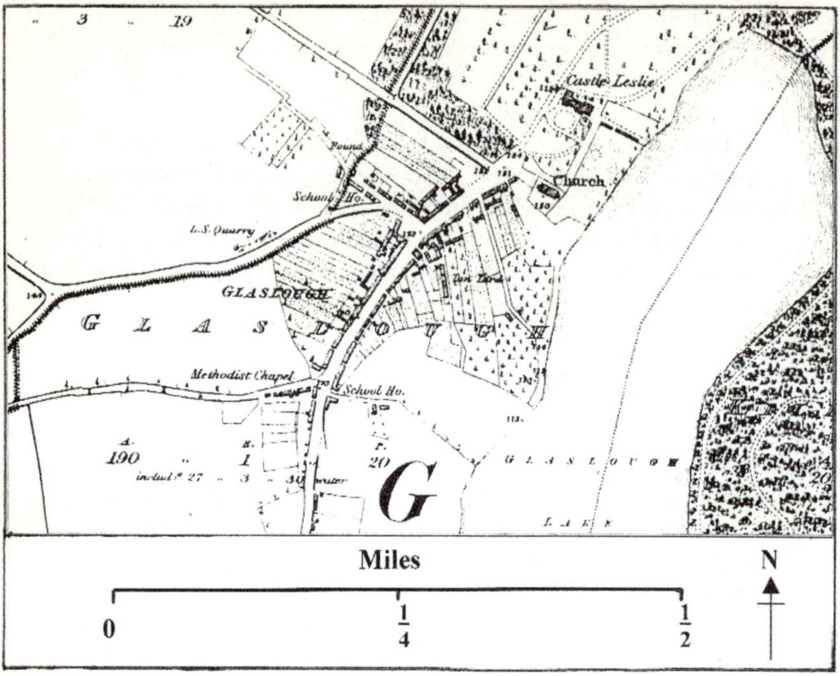

4. The town of Glaslough, 1835

1821 census recorded 535 persons living in 118 houses in Emyvale and 847 persons living in 177 houses in Glaslough.[65] The population growth continued at Emyvale throughout the period of this study.[66] In 1838 the village was described as consisting 'of one street . . . The houses are regular. They consist of 67 of 1-story and 57 of 2; of these only 3 are slated. They are for the most part built of stone.'[67] In 1801, Coote described Glaslough as having 'a striking engaging appearance, and some excellent slated houses, two stories high, but at present it has no trade'.[68] When the ordnance survey visited Glaslough in the 1830s, it had '1 principal street and a smaller one which runs off from near the centre of the main street. The houses in general are good. There have been many new houses lately built by Mrs Leslie. They are of stone, slated. The town consists of 32 houses of 1, 45 of 2 and 7 of 3-storys; 29 of these are thatched and the remainder slated.'[69] The modern development of Glaslough at this time is illustrated by Gailey, who has shown that in the 1830s the further west one went in the north of Ireland the percentage of thatch dwellings increased, but that Glaslough was an exception to this having only 35 per cent thatched houses.[70] This he explains was owing to the influence of the Leslies in improving the living conditions of their tenants. In the town the traders and occupations included: woollen merchants/drapers, hardware merchants, grocers, whiskey dealers, a doctor, a tallow chandler, a delph merchant, one painter and glazier, two shoemakers, two smiths, and three places of accommodation and entertainment.[71] In addition to the two schools in Glaslough the commissioners of public instruction identified six other day schools, a Sunday school and six hedge schools in the parish educating over 1,000 pupils in the 1830s.[72]

Although Glaslough and Emyvale were important centres in the community, their population never exceeded 14 per cent of the parish's population before the Famine.[73] The industries in the parish such as those described by Lewis, Coote and in the ordnance survey memoirs, were primarily an adjunct to the parish's agricultural economy. The predominant occupation of most people in the parish was linked to rural agriculture. The census of 1821, 1831 and 1841 give an indication of how people in the parish were employed in the early nineteenth century. However, one of the problems with these census is the inconsistencies between how they classified people's occupations. For example, the 1831 census only classified the occupations of men, while the 1821 census made no distinction between the occupations of men or women and grouped them all under the one heading, persons. Bearing this in mind these census provide an indication of the occupations pursued by people in the parish of Donagh and how this community lived. Table 3 summarises some of the information recorded by the census.

Table 3. Occupations in the parish of Donagh, 1821, 1831, 1841

Chief Occupations	1821		1831		1841	
	Persons	*Percentage*	*Families*	*Percentage*	*Families*	*Percentage*
Agriculture	1,108	21.5	1,422	68.3	1,351	69.7
Trade, manufacture & handicrafts	3,242	63.0	246	11.8	450	23.2
Others	800	15.5	414	19.9	138	7.1
Total	5,150	100.0	2,082	100.0	1,939	100.0

Source: Census of Ireland 1821, 1831 and 1841.

The table indicates a change between 1821 and 1831 from occupations based on trade, manufacture and handicrafts to agricultural occupations. This probably represents a change in how the people's occupations were perceived. In 1821 people were still viewed as primarily involved in linen manufacture, whereas with the continuing changes in the linen industry by 1831 people were perceived as primarily involved in agriculture. This confusion in classification is illustrated in Thomas Johnston's reply to the poor inquiry in the 1830s where he interchanged the classifications weaver, labourer and farmer. He responded to one question stating that due to the depression in the linen industry, the great body of weavers had become labourers and in another reply he stated that the inhabitants being principally weavers, their farms were generally small.[74] The 1841 census confirmed this change in how occupations were perceived, agriculture having become predominant. This census also provided details of the occupations of both males and females. 1,636 males from Donagh were categorised as 'ministering to food', representing 78 per cent of the males in occupations in the parish.[75] 1,054 females from Donagh were categorised as 'ministering to clothing', which represented 75 per cent of the parish's females in occupations. These categories were subdivided at county level. 75 per cent of the county's men were either farmers or labourers, both in the 'ministering to food' category.[76] 72 per cent of the county's women worked as spinners of either flax or wool, which is in the 'ministering to clothing' category. Therefore, between 1800 and 1841, with the change in the linen industry, men moved away from occupations associated with the linen industry and became predominantly farmers or agricultural labourers. Women continued to spin, which supplemented the family's income. However, when categorised by family, the 1841 census viewed families in the parish as being predominantly involved in agriculture, the man's occupation.

This census data reflects the changes in the linen industry during these years. With the introduction of power driven machinery into the spinning industry from the late eighteenth century, initially for coarse products but later for fine yarn, home spun yarn became uneconomical.[77] Further, mill-spun yarn was quicker and easier to weave so that it was extended to family members rather than just the men of the household. These spinning mills were located in the towns and cities of Ireland, Scotland and England making the industry non-local and exposing it to international competitive forces.[78] In County Monaghan the impact of these technological changes and the globalisation of this industry led to the restructuring of the household domestic linen industry, which became concentrated at the ends of the production chain. Flax growing was pursued by the men and weaving, organised by putting-out manufacturers, was carried on by the women and young boys or girls of the family. Thus the household retained its multiple labour involvement increasing its output to offset the lost earnings from spinning and the decreasing earnings of weavers.

The parish's community traded the produce of their labours at fairs and markets. At the beginning of the nineteenth century there were no market towns in Donagh. Monaghan and Armagh were the most significant market towns nearby. From 1806 there was a monthly fair on the third Friday of each month at Glaslough, which replaced the three annual fairs held there prior to this.[79] By the 1830s there was also a weekly market held on a Friday for wheat and flax.[80] Throughout these years custom free fairs were held at Emyvale.[81] In addition to venues for trade, fairs were also social events. William Carleton who lived in the neighbourhood of Emyvale in the early nineteenth century described a typical fair in his story *The fair of Emyvale*, where after the business there were festivities, which included everything from 'pitch-and-toss to manslaughter.'[82] An extract from his story gives an impression of what a fair was like:[83]

> The fair, of course, was a moving mass of animation, and occasionally of uproar; the latter produced by the shouting of men and the bellowings of startled cattle, as the parties conducting them came into contact with each other while passing in the street. But after the pressing business of the day had been principally concluded, the crowd, especially the young of both sexes, might be observed, in connexion with their friends and relatives, to devote more of their time to pleasure and conviviality.

Faction fights also broke out at fairs, which according to Carleton occurred on the conclusion of the day's business and then they 'were on a large and comprehensive scale'. Some of these fights probably reflected the sectarian tensions within the community. Seymour Leslie recounts stories of some of these attacks including one at the Emyvale fair in 1813, where he states a number of men were killed and the attackers were acquitted.[84] In his autobiography Charles Gavan Duffy recalls sectarian tensions, in his youth, in north Monaghan in the first half of the nineteenth century: 'The Orange drum was heard on every hill from June till late August to celebrate the Boyne and Aughrim'.[85] These divisions were also present in the parish of Donagh, where a large Protestant community sharing the fears and insecurities of their co-religionists in the neighbouring counties had established two Orange lodges in Glaslough by 1798.[86] Initially, the Orange lodges had been established primarily in response to the spread of radicalism and republicanism. The United Irishmen had been active in the Glaslough area in 1797. In April a number of armed men 'plundered many houses of arms, and committed other enormities there'.[87] However, the Glaslough area was quiet in 1798, probably because the United Irish leaders in the area had been arrested in the previous year.[88] In the early nineteenth century the divide between Catholic and Protestant communities in the parish is illustrated in the number of inter-denominational marriages at Glennan Presbyterian meeting house.[89] Between 1805 and 1821 there were forty-one marriages between Presbyterians and established church Protestants, while there were only four marriages between Presbyterians and Catholics. For one of these, on 28 September 1815, between John Pegan and Sarah M'Court, the minister expressed his views of Catholicism in the register writing that she 'renounced the errors of the Church of Rome'.[90] Protestant dominance at local level was reinforced in 1816 when the all Protestant cadre of the Monaghan militia were quartered in a large house in the centre of Glaslough.[91] Leslie, as colonel, ordered that they were to parade on Wednesdays and Fridays and to march to church on Sundays with their band. On the twenty-fourth day of each month they paraded with full kit.[92] The pageantry of these Protestant parades in the locality provided regular celebrations of loyalty to Britain and her victories. Further, Dublin Castle entrusted this Protestant military unit with security responsibilities for the local community, when in November 1817 they ordered Leslie to disband the local corps of yeomanry.[93]

At the beginning of the nineteenth century the local economy on the Leslies' estates in north Monaghan conformed to a proto-industrialised model typical of most of Ulster. However, the linen industry changed in Donagh as it did elsewhere in Ireland with the family household production unit being forced into the ends of the production chain, flax growth and weaving, thus narrowing their sources of earnings, which were now increasingly a function of the global linen business. Coupled with this development there was a major recession in Ireland after the end of the Napoleonic wars. These developments led to significant financial difficulties for landed estate businesses and also to a decline in the living conditions for their communities. The following chapters in this pamphlet will examine how Charles Powell Leslie II managed his estate at Glaslough and how the lives of the people living on this estate changed between 1800 and 1841.

The business of managing a landed estate

The estate inherited by Charles Powell Leslie II from his father (figure 5) was free from family settlements, as his mother had pre-deceased her husband and the marriage settlement between his father and step-mother in 1785 was not secured on any of the estates.[1] This freedom from encumbrances gave Leslie considerable advantages in developing and expanding his landed estate business.

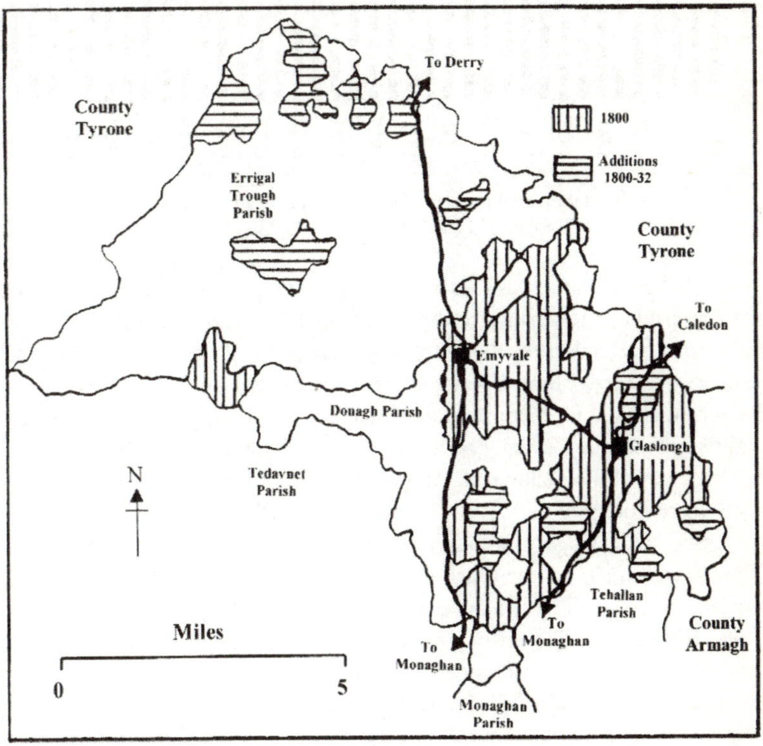

5. Map of Charles Powell Leslie II's estates in the parishes of Donagh and Errigal Trough, County Monaghan

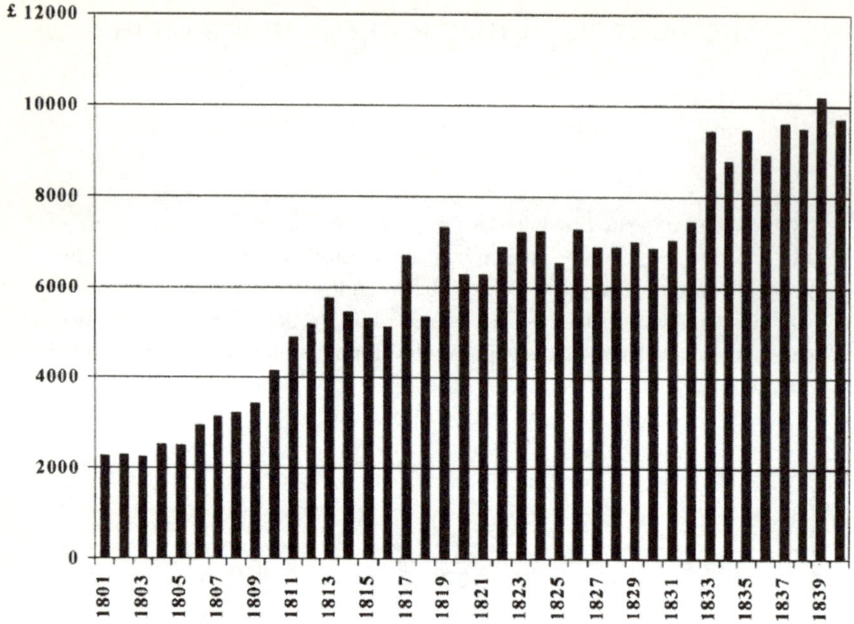

6. Rental income from the Leslie estates at Glaslough, 1801–40
Source: C.L.A., D1, D1A; N.L.I., Ms 5813

Landed estates were businesses whose revenues primarily came from rental incomes paid by the tenants for their holdings. In the early nineteenth century, the tenure agreements for these holdings were generally held under a lease for years or lives, or without a lease, referred to as held at will. In the latter case the rent was fixed for a year and thus could change each year. During the late eighteenth century there had been a general trend away from leases to holdings at will. This allowed landlords to increase their rental income in line with economic growth. Figure 6 shows the growth in the rental income for the Leslies' estates near Glaslough, from £2,263 in 1800 to £10,508 in 1840. These estates included the Glaslough, Emyvale, Hutcheson, Montgomery and the Moore estates. The last three estates were bought during Charles Powell Leslie II's lifetime. The initial growth commenced after 1803 following the renewal of war between France and Britain. This war increased the demand for Irish agricultural produce, which was further stimulated in 1807 by Napoleon's strategy of closing the European markets to British trade, referred to as the continental system. His aim was to ruin British industry and to induce a state of economic difficulty and social unrest among the British public. The British campaign against France in the Iberian Peninsula, which commenced at this time and continued until 1814 added further demand for Irish produce. The consequential boom in the Irish economy allowed landlords to increase their rental income from holdings without a lease or whose lease had expired, as tenants were able to pay more. The continued growth in the Irish population further stimulated the demand for land and thus also put upward pressure on rents.

As none of his estates were encumbered in family settlements, Charles Powell Leslie II was able to invest his increased earnings and expand his landed estate business. The purchase of the Montgomery estate, primarily located in the parish of Donagh and the neighbouring parish of Errigal Trough, added to Leslie's rental income in 1810.[2] By 1811, Leslie had doubled his revenue from his estates near Glaslough since the commencement of the war in 1803. The rental income continued to increase up until 1813, peaking at £5,758, before falling slightly in 1814. The end of this period of growth in rental income was probably as a consequence of the slowing down in Ireland's economy with declining demand, following Napoleon's first abdication and the end of the war in Europe. The rental arrears in November 1814 at £216 were the highest since 1803.[3] The economic recession in Ireland, which commenced at this time, led to dropping agricultural prices and a decline in living standards. The price of oats, the most important grain grown in the parish of Donagh, dropped by about 11 per cent in the five years after the end of the war and never reached its wartime prices in the following twenty years (table 4).[4]

Table 4. Index numbers of Dublin market prices for oats, 1812–40 (base 1812–15 = 100)

Average for years	1812–15	1816–20	1821–5	1826–30	1831–5	1836–40
Index number	100	89	68	80	62	76

Source: J.S. Donnelly, *The land and the people of nineteenth-century Cork* (London, 1975), p. 45.

By 1815, as the national recession deepened, the local economy in north County Monaghan suffered consequentially. Arrears rose to £1,667 on these estates near Glaslough, as tenants had difficulties in paying their rents.[5] The rental income from the recently acquired Hutcheson estate, £211 for the half year ending in November 1815, contributed to making up some of this lost income. This estate of the four adjacent townlands, Annabog, Corraghdown, Drumnoland and Teledon, close to Glaslough, contained over 318 acres.[6] In 1816 the local economy continued to decline and the arrears on the Glaslough and Emyvale estates reached £2,519 by November of that year, which equated to over 50 per cent of its annual rental income.[7] These difficulties in the local economy persisted until 1824 before the arrears reached manageable levels, when the Glaslough and Emyvale arrears were 10 per cent of the annual rent on the estate.[8] During these uncertain times, Leslie managed to increase his overall rental income primarily through estate acquisition. In general the rental income increased only marginally on these individual estates indicating that the rent charged per acre was reasonably stable.[9] In July 1822 he added to the Glaslough, Emyvale, Hutcheson and Montgomery estates when he bought the Moore estate located partially in the parish of Errigal Trough, County Monaghan and partially in County Tyrone.[10]

Throughout the remainder of his life Leslie maintained his income at these levels and kept his estates' arrears to manageable levels. The recession of 1825–6 appears not to have had as significant an impact on these north Monaghan estates as the earlier post-war slump. Cash was used to pay rents on the Leslie estates in the late eighteenth century and it is probable, like most of Ulster, this practice continued into the nineteenth century thus insulating the local economy from the banking collapse in Ireland in the early 1820s.[11] The rental income dropped again in 1832 and arrears increased.[12] This probably reflects the impact on the management of the estates of Charles Powell Leslie II's death. As his eldest son was still a minor, Charles Powell Leslie II's widow, Christina, managed the estates through her husband's agents. By 1833, income from the estates was restored to previous levels. The rental income from the estates gradually increased during the 1830s. However, arrears were higher than when Charles Powell Leslie II had been alive. It was not until 1839 that the arrears on the Glaslough and Emyvale estates again dropped below 10 per cent of the annual rent on these estates.[13]

From 1800 to 1841, the period of this study, the Leslies employed a number of agents and solicitors in the management and administration of their estates. These men managed the estates on a daily basis, collected the rentals, pursued the arrears and executed the Leslies' policy and decisions. They thus played a key role in the growth of the Leslies landed estate business and occupied an influential position in the life of the estate's community. The Leslies' solicitors during this period were Blayney Owen Mitchell in Monaghan and Robert Borrowes in Dublin. Table 5 lists their agents.

The first of these, John Rawdon, succeeded his uncle, John Dollard who had been agent to Robert Leslie for many years, in 1753.[14] Rawdon was agent for the Glaslough and Emyvale estates during the minority of Charles Powell Leslie I and he was retained in this role when Charles Powell Leslie I came of age in 1761. He was also appointed as agent for the Pettigo estate, County Donegal, in 1777. In 1800 his half-yearly salary for the Glaslough and Emyvale estates was £25 and for the Pettigo estate he received £37.[15] John Rawdon was an important person in the Donagh community with holdings in 1799 that included mills in Kilcran and Stramore, the shambles in Glaslough, a tenement in Glaslough, and land in Aughnagap, Coolcalida, Doagheys, Kilcran, Tullyree and Legar Hill, paying a total annual rent of over £148.[16] However, following a dispute with Charles Powell Leslie II over the accounts, which culminated in a court action in 1806, he was replaced by Robert

Table 5. List of agents on the Leslie estates in Counties Monaghan, Tyrone, and Donegal, 1800–41

John Rawdon	Agent for the Glaslough & Emyvale estates, Co. Monaghan	1751–1802/03
	Agent for the Pettigo estate, Co. Donegal	1777–1802/03
Robert Murdock	Agent for the Glaslough & Emyvale estates, Co. Monaghan	1802/03–22
	Agent for the Montgomery estate, Co. Monaghan	1810–22
	Agent for the Hutcheson estate, Co. Monaghan	1815–22
William Murdock	Agent for the Glaslough, Emyvale, Montgomery and Hutcheson estates, Co. Monaghan	From 1822
	Accountant for the Glaslough, Emyvale, Montgomery, Hutcheson, Garvey, Lower Trough and Pettigo estates	From 1832
John Aiken	Agent for the Pettigo estate, Co. Donegal	1802/03–16
James Nixon	Agent for the Cordoo estate, Co. Monaghan	From 1815/16
	Agent for the Pettigo estate, Co. Donegal	From 1816
John Ross	Agent for the Lower Trough estate, Co. Monaghan	From 1822
	Agent for the Garvey estate, Co. Tyrone	From 1822

Murdock as agent for the Glaslough and Emyvale estates and by John Aiken as agent for the Pettigo estate in either 1802 or 1803.[17] In his affidavit in his defence, in the court case, Rawdon referred to himself as being 'honoured with the confidence, and approbation' of Charles Powell Leslie I, having served him to the 'best of his judgement, and ability faithfully, and honestly'.[18] This provides an insight into the desirable elements in a relationship between landlord and agent of honesty, faithfulness, trust and friendship. This dispute arose following Charles Powell Leslie I's death when it was discovered that there was a debt of over £2,000 owed by Rawdon to his employer. Rawdon explained, in his affidavit, that during the insurgent activity in 1797, his house in Glaslough was raided. Three arms were stolen and some papers and vouchers were destroyed including records of his financial transactions in managing the estate, which was why the accounts were in dispute. However, his former employer's accounts and the estates' bank accounts, when examined, still left a shortfall in what he owed the Leslies. After the case Leslie took possession of Rawdon's property in Glaslough indicating that Rawdon lost.[19] The following extract from a letter, which Rawdon wrote to his wife,

'Bel', in October 1793, from Pettigo, reveals some of his responsibilities, the large amounts of money he handled, the processes in his work and provides an insight into the life of an agent in late eighteenth century and early nineteenth-century Ireland:[20]

> I am not likely to get away from this country for some days yet . . . There is a cursed same trouble-some tenant here called Wm Swanston (*sic*), he has been my plague for years. On Thursday next his interest under Mr Leslie is to be sold by the sheriff in Lifford there I must attend to claim £10 2*s.* 0*d.* claiming one years rent due by him for which I must make an application before the sheriff which no other person could do. I must leave this morrow and I do not expect to get back here sooner than Friday as the sale is to be at two o'clock on Thursday evening at the courthouse . . . I have not heard of you since I got here three weeks this day.
>
> I propose sending off McKenna to G[lasloug]h to morrow morning. I expected he shall be with you tomorrow night. He carrys one parcel containing nine packets . . . in all £460 9*s.* 0*d.* also sixty guineas of silver in three packets of twenty each.
>
> If all gets safe, open the gold packet take out No.1, 2, 3, & 4 in all £200 4*s.* 0*d.* Send for Ned McC and tell him I request he may go to Armagh with it on Thursday to Dr Morrison, to whom I beg you may write by Ned requesting he may get it sent off to his brother by first opportunity, in safe hands
>
> Send 10 Gs. to Js. Connally, 10 to Wm Smal, 10 to Mr Mollan, and 10 to Mr. Crookshank and give Ned McC 10 until I can settle.

From the time of his appointment, Robert Murdock, Rawdon's successor, carried out the daily duties as agent of the Glaslough and Emyvale estates. He corresponded with Charles Powell Leslie II regularly. A letter written to Leslie on 3 December 1817 included the following extracts which reveals the nature of his work:[21]

> I have gone through the wood with Mr Smyth and I enclose you a return of what trees we found down by the winds I will in a little time get a return of any he has on hands unsold . . . the flax is something higher in our markets perhaps it would be best to try what yours would sell at there is about one hundred stone of it . . . I have told John Reid that you have desired Wm. Close should have liberty of shooting the demesne he says it was never better loaded with game of all kinds and that there was not one shot fired in it this season.

This type of correspondence ensured that Leslie was informed about his estates at Glaslough, the community and developments in the county such as market prices. Further correspondence from Robert Murdock on 26 January 1819 reveals that Leslie maintained control of decisions relating to the selection of his tenants. Murdock writes requesting Leslie's instructions 'there is parts of Mullencallog not yet tenanted I enclose you a copy of three proposed I have for it which if you approve of I will give them the land.'[22] These letters reveal the attention paid by Leslie to his estates even when he was away from them. He maintained control of the business in his hands only delegating limited authority to his agents, who were expected to act according the instructions he gave them. Robert Murdock does not appear to have acquired the wealth of his predecessor, John Rawdon. In 1799 he held a tenement in Glaslough and two parks in the townland of Lisgo, paying a yearly rent of £10 5*s*.[23] By 1823 he held land in the townlands of Drumbanagher, Trynany, Lisgo, Tullyree and a tenement in Glaslough, paying a half-yearly rent of £15 4*s*. 4½*d*.[24] He appears to have been a respected member of the local community, which he was active in, serving as churchwarden and participating in the Church of Ireland vestry meetings.[25] His son William took over his role as agent in 1822. Robert Murdock continues to appear as a tenant in the rent rolls and thus he probably retired. There is no evidence in Leslie's correspondence indicating that he was dissatisfied with Robert Murdock's work.

William Murdock succeeded his father as agent for the estates near Glaslough in 1822.[26] He had assisted his father prior to this, in particular when his father was ill in 1818.[27] This experience gave him a good understanding of the work of an agent and particular knowledge with regard to the Leslie estates. He continued the agent's role in a similar manner to his father. The following letter to Leslie of 20 October 1831 is typical of his correspondence:[28]

> There has been a man looking at Emy mill he has offered £50 a year for the mill and four acres of land. He is a miller ... and would repair the mill at his own expense ... I think as you would be put to no expense further in repairs it would be as advantageous to give it to him. I am draining the bog bottoms at the rear of Cloncaw next Donagh and preparing them to lay them down for meadow ... The wheat and Potatos crop is very good the oats but very middling butter and beef is selling very well I think the tenants will pay their rents well this year ... You will please say what your wishes are about the mill he has offered security in the rent.

This letter of William Murdock, with his father's correspondence, reaffirms how Leslie maintained control of the management of his estates and kept in touch with local developments. William Murdock was also active in both local and county communities. He served as a churchwarden in the parish of Donagh, was secretary to the committee for the Glaslough and Emyvale dispensary and was a member of the grand jury.[29] The Leslies appear to have been happy with his work as he acted as main accountant for Glaslough, Emyvale, Montgomery, Hutcheson, Moore and Pettigo estates after Charles Powell Leslie II's death, signing off on the other agents accounts and consolidating the individual estate accounts into one account.[30]

Little correspondence exists describing the work of John Aiken, the agent for the Pettigo estate. However, he returned large arrears in the accounts from September 1814 without providing details of the tenants who had fallen into arrears.[31] It later transpired that there was sums of money missing from the Pettigo estate's accounts. James Nixon replaced Aiken in 1816, when Aiken's financial affairs with Charles Powell Leslie II had become disputed.

James Nixon was appointed as paymaster in the Monaghan militia in June 1798.[32] He fought alongside Leslie during the 1798 rebellion and served under him during the war years when the militia was on active service. Following the disbanding of the Monaghan militia in March 1816, Nixon was retained on the permanent staff, the unit's cadre.[33] Nixon was appointed agent for the small Cordoo estate, 120 acres in County Monaghan, when it was purchased in either 1815 or 1816, additionally he took up the same duties on the Pettigo estate in 1816.[34] Like Leslie's other agents, Nixon's correspondence kept Leslie informed regarding his estates. However, his correspondence also provided Leslie with information relating to opportunities to buy additional lands. He researched the valuation of these lands and recommended whether Leslie should buy them. In a typical note in this regard in April 1815 Nixon wrote:[35]

> You will perceive by the rent roll of Coote's lands, of which you are the purchaser, that Mr. Ley of Leyboro had a lease of Cordoo for two lives yet in being, this lease I am informed he made anew to his second son Francis Ley who has again set them to a man called John Lane, If I am well informed (should your purchase be confirmed) you might purchase both their interests on easy terms, as I have now an execution against Ley's goods and Lane has got into a chancery suit with his late landlord Mr. J. Coote, which will very probably leave him in the same situation, should you wish I shall make enquiries.
>
> I think you should point out to Mr. Borrowes that Coote has sold many annuities and that he should therefore be cautious that none of them were secured on those lands.

In another letter in June 1824 Nixon wrote to Leslie and informed him about the intended sale of Colonel Gore's property.[36] Leslie appears to have relied on Nixon in this role of analysing potential properties for purchase. As an agent, Nixon appears to have been tough, diligent and attentive to his work. In his letter of July 1823 from Pettigo he wrote 'there never were so many difficulties in the way of the people making up their arrears . . . But I shall stick to them until I get all they have (if possible) from them.'[37] However, he could also be pragmatic as in his letter from Glaslough in April 1824 regarding the Pettigo estate, 'There is still a considerable arrear of the gale, but I know they could not pay it off, until their cattle get into better condition for the May fair.'[38] Again in April 1831 he wrote regarding the difficulty of collecting the Pettigo rentals, owing to the poverty in the country, stating it was useless to impound cattle as there were no prices to be had for them. He recommended 'The only chance for the landlord is in my opinion to leave the cows with the poor tenants to make butter and little else can be had until harvest.'[39] In June 1831 he wrote to Leslie 'The tenants don't look for any relief from subscriptions all they require is a little bit longer time than usual to pay their rents and I am convinced you will have no objection to accede to.'[40] Leslie appears to have adopted Nixon's recommendation as Nixon wrote to him in July 1831 informing him 'that the forthcoming crops will enable your tenantry to repay you with blessings for your indulgence.'[41]

Charles Powell Leslie II had worked with James Nixon for many years and clearly established a trusted friendship. Nixon was entrusted with buying a jaunting car for Leslie in 1822.[42] When Leslie travelled to County Monaghan from England for the assizes, he stayed with Nixon rather than at Castle Leslie.[43] After Leslie's death in 1831, Nixon continued to work for Mrs Leslie. His role as militia paymaster reveals that Nixon had administrative skills and was familiar with accounts. His correspondence with Leslie also reveals that he had knowledge of the law, in particular as it related to land ownership and he also understood land valuation. He may have had a legal qualification. Leslie used these skills by employing Nixon in more varied roles than his fellow agents. James Nixon was a signatory to the letter from the 'Landed proprietors and the gentlemen of County Monaghan' addressed to Charles Powell Leslie II, following the latter's election defeat of 1826.[44] The other signatories included some of the largest landlords in the county including Matthew Anketell, John Madden, C.A. Leslie and Thomas Singleton. This letter shows that Nixon moved in the same society as the Leslies and other landed gentry being viewed as a gentleman, a position in society supported by his military background and his obvious education. Further, the letter attacked the Catholic clergy and Catholic Association's involvement in the recent election as threatening the county's 'independence' revealing Nixon's opposition to the emancipation movement.

Captain John Ross was originally from Scotland. He was born around 1779. In 1814 he was the adjudant in the Monaghan regiment of militia with twenty years service, previously having served in the regular army.[45] He was a close friend to Leslie before becoming his agent witnessing the baptism of the son and heir of Charles Powell Leslie II and his wife Christina on 21 November 1821.[46] In 1823 when Ross married Mary Marsh at Glaslough, Leslie witnessed the marriage.[47] Ross also witnessed the baptism of the some of Leslie's other children notably in 1823, the future first baronet, John, and in 1825, Prudence

Penelope.[48] Ross was appointed agent of the Moore estate, located in the parish of Errigal Trough, County Monaghan, and County Tyrone, in 1822 following its purchase in that year.[49] The Moore estate was also referred to as the Lower Trough and Garvey estates. John Ross continued in this role throughout the period of this study. Little correspondence exists related to this estate during these years. The small amount of correspondence, all post 1831, indicates that he was attentive to duties. The Leslie family were satisfied with his work as he was retained as agent after Charles Powell Leslie II's death. As a retired army officer Ross was able to move in the same society as the Leslies and bore the character of a gentlemen. Like his fellow agent, James Nixon, Ross was also a signatory to the letter from the 'Landed proprietors and gentlemen of the county of Monaghan' in June 1826 addressed to Leslie, aligning Ross with its anti-Catholic emancipation sentiments.[50]

Robert Borrowes was Leslie's solicitor in Dublin. He was not only a business associate, he was also a trusted friend and relative of Leslie. He married Leslie's niece, Charlotte Madden of Hilton on 22 December 1805.[51] Borrowes was a trustee in the marriage settlement between Leslie and his second wife Christina Fosberry. The other trustees were family members including Leslie's brother, John, bishop of Dromore.[52]

Blayney Owen Mitchell was the Monaghan solicitor used by Charles Powell Leslie throughout this period providing legal representation for local issues, such as acting on behalf of Leslie in the legal process required to eject a tenant. He also appears to have kept Leslie informed of local Monaghan politics such as in April 1810 when he wrote 'I am heartily glad to hear you are determined to soon return to Glaslough. Your friends often felt your absence. Mr. Dawson has been in the county of Monaghan for some time back taking his share of what has been going forward.'[53]

Leslie's agents and solicitors were men of varied backgrounds and qualifications. The most important qualities required by Leslie appears to have been trust and honesty. Both Rawdon and Aiken were sacked when trust broke down with regard to their management of the estates financial affairs. Leslie was uncompromising when his employees did not perform as required. Rawdon, who had worked for the family for over fifty years, serving Leslie's grandmother and father, and who pleaded for clemency in his affidavit in 1806, was not tolerated by Leslie because of his dishonesty. Leslie did not replace Rawdon with a single agent, perhaps because it gave one agent too much influence or perhaps because the Monaghan estates were too distant from the Donegal estate for both to be managed effectively by one person. Leslie's preference was to employ relatives and friends in senior roles in the management of his estates, probably because he trusted them more. Social acceptability also appears to have been important. Both Ross and Nixon were men with military backgrounds with experience in positions of authority making them suitable to represent Leslie and likely to command respect amongst peers and tenants. Borrowes was related to Leslie by marriage and thus a peer. It is probable that all Leslie's senior employees were members of the Church of Ireland. Ross, Borrowes, Robert and William Murdock were all Church of Ireland Protestants. It is probable that Nixon, an opponent of Catholic Emancipation, was also a Church of Ireland Protestant. Additionally, Leslie's agents were required to have knowledge of the business and an extensive knowledge of the country. Nixon appears to have excelled in his knowledge of developments in County Monaghan. The accounts, which all these men kept, show that they were educated and some had professional expertise.

These agents collected the rents from the tenants who held their land on Leslie's estates as agreed in the contract, the lease, one of the central items in the landlord-tenant relationship. Leslie's tenants had either leases for lives, years or some had no lease. The administration of the leases was one of the key activities on a nineteenth-century estate. The Leslies had owned the Glaslough and Emyvale estates since the seventeenth century and therefore had established and implemented the leasing policy and agreed all the leases on these estates. Analysis of these leases provides an insight into their approach. Unfortunately the quantity of surviving leases is small because a large number were destroyed in recent years.[54] However, other manuscripts amongst the Leslie papers, like rent rolls, help to reveal the Leslies' approach to leases. The rent roll for the year ending 1799 lists the tenure types on the estates at the beginning of the nineteenth century and these are summarised in table 6.

The fee farms were leases granted in the early eighteenth century by Dean John Leslie to prominent gentry settlers.[55] The holdings that these leases relate

Table 6. Summary of types of tenure in the rent rolls for the Glaslough and Emyvale estates, County Monaghan, for the year end 1799

Lease Type	Glaslough Town	Glaslough estate (excluding the town)	Emyvale estate	Total
Fee Farms	0	12	0	12
Lease for lives renewable	14	1	2	17
3 Life Leases	5	34	63	102
4 Life Leases	0	0	1	1
Lease for lives (Number of lives not recorded)	0	2	0	2
No Lease/At will	11	26	10	47
Total	**30**	**75**	**76**	**181**
Partnership leases	0	3	6	9

Source: Glaslough & Emyvale Rentals (C.L.A., D1).

to were thus effectively sold and are not relevant when analysing the Leslies' approach to leases in the early nineteenth century. Tenants were most likely to have a three life lease, which was the most common type of tenure on the estate in 1799. Tenant at will was the next most common tenure type. In terms of the distribution of these tenure types on the different parts of the estate, the Leslies gave a lease for lives renewable most frequently to tenants taking holdings in their demesne town of Glaslough. This type of tenure was very attractive to tenants. Using this policy the Leslies could be selective and ensure that they had preferred tenants settled in Glaslough town. The only lease for lives renewable on the Glaslough estate, outside of the town, was given to the agent, John Rawdon. The two leases for lives renewable on the Emyvale estate were given to prominent middlemen, Thomas Benson for the town of Emyvale and John Charlton for part of Tully. Benson's lease was the one that Charles Powell Leslie I, who was encouraging the establishment of a Protestant linen weaving community in the locality, had originally given to William Ogle. Leases for lives predominated on the Emyvale estate, whereas tenants at will were more common on the Glaslough estate and were also significant in the town of Glaslough. The rental income from the Emyvale estate had increased rapidly during the 1760s surpassing the revenue contribution made to the Leslies by the Glaslough estate's rental income, which only increased slowly in these years.[56] It is probable that most of the leases for lives on the Emyvale estate date from this time, whereas the Glaslough estates' leases had been given in earlier years, thus limiting its growth in contributing rental revenue in the 1760s. Once the lives in these leases had expired in the late eighteenth century no lease appears to have been given to the tenants, who held their land at will subsequently.

These 1799 tenure agreements were those which Charles Powell Leslie II inherited with these estates in 1800. They were the initial tenure agreements which he used to manage the estate and whose conditions he was obliged to respect and implement. The 1803 rent rolls provide some additional comments on types of tenure, which provide an initial indication of the changes Leslie made to tenure arrangements.[57] Alexander Widney who had a holding in Killykeady on the Emyvale estate was recorded as having a lease for three lives in the 1799 rent roll. In 1803 his holding was recorded as having no lease. William Crookshanks, a middleman, held a lease for three lives for his holding of Drumturk in 1799. In 1803 this holding was leased to ten individual tenants each recorded as having no lease. The 1803 rent rolls also reveal the break up of the partnership leases of Cormick McAtee & Partners who held land at will in Killykeady in 1799. In 1803 each tenant at will was identified individually. Similarly, Francis Kelly's partnership for the holding of Mullan in 1799 had broken up by 1803. Thus within three years of inheriting these estates, Leslie had replaced a number of leases for lives with tenure agreements where the tenant held their land at will, without a lease. He also showed a preference to by-pass middlemen and partnerships and established direct tenure agreements with his tenants himself.

However, Leslie did not abandon the use of leases. In 1810 he leased a house and tenement to John Diven, a blacksmith, 'for and during the life of the said John Diven the lessee'.[58] John Aiken, Leslie's agent for the Donegal estate, sent a note to Leslie stating his understanding of Leslie's instructions for leases, which he was required to implement. In these instructions the conditions were specified and the term of the leases was twenty years.[59] In 1834 the lease for the towns and lands of Skernageeragh commonly known as Emyvale was renewed between Leslie's wife, Christina, and Richard Benson, as all three lives in the previous lease were deceased.[60] Leslie's approach appears to have been dependent on the case in question. John Diven, a blacksmith, provided an important service to the community and his holding was located in the demesne village, Glaslough, where the Leslies had given good terms to their tenants. Richard Benson a middleman whose family had been reliable tenants for over thirty years was a good tenant to retain in the depressed 1830s. The holdings where Leslie had replaced leases for lives, with tenure agreements where the tenants were at will, were all rural farm holdings. This approach allowed Leslie to benefit from the demand for land in the early nineteenth century, which drove rents upwards. Simultaneously, Leslie gave leases to tenants who added strategic value to the development of his estates' towns and lands, with either their skills or money.

The selection of the lives for leases was done carefully. If the tenant were fortunate to have a life in the lease of a young person, who lived a long life, they would have the same rent for many years. One of the difficulties for the landlord was knowing when a life in a lease had died, particularly in the nineteenth century when people moved from the locality or emigrated. Therefore, prominent individuals were often selected as the lives in the leases. This practice was followed on the Leslie estates at Glaslough as is illustrated in table 7. For leases held in perpetuity, also referred to as leases for lives renewable, the lives selected were those of the royal family. Notice of the death of a member of the royal family was easily ascertained. However, for leases for lives and years or for lives only, family members of either the tenant or the landlord or local people known to the family and the landlord appear to have been chosen. It was difficult for a landlord to keep track of such lives, especially when the individual named as the life moved away from north Monaghan to Dublin or in some cases America. This table illustrates one of the routine activities associated with administering an estate tracking the lives and years for each of the leases, as once a lease expired, the landlord had the opportunity to increase his earnings by renewing it for a higher rent or replacing a difficult tenant. In March 1818 William Murdock wrote to Leslie on behalf of his father Robert, Leslie's agent, to inform him of the death of 'Mr. Irvine the life of the lease of Annagh'.[61] He asked Leslie for 'directions before he takes possession of it

Table 7. Status of lives in some leases for holdings on the Glaslough & Emyvale estates, *c.*1789–1810[62]

Townland	*Tenure*	*Tenants Name*	*Lives of Leases*	*Observations*
Glaslough	Perpetuity	Wm. Young	Prince of Wales Prince Frederick Prince William	First second and third sons of his Majesty
Glaslough	Lives & years	Wm. Hamilton	Wm. Hamilton Lessee Joseph Marshall Robert Lines	Dead, Years done Dead In Caledon
New Mills & Stramore	Lives & years	John Rawdon Esq.	Matthew Anketell Nath. Montgomery Elizb. Henderson	
Trynany	Lives and years	Wm. Johnston	Wm. Johnston Wm. Johnston Robt. Cochrane	Dead In Dublin In America
Glaslough & Clanca	Lives only	John Irwin	John Irwin Wm. Cochran Charles Ferguson	Dead Dead In America

Note: Wm. Hamilton's lease in Glaslough was for lives and years. This meant that Wm. Hamilton's lease was for a number of years, typically twenty-one years, or three lives whichever was the greater. Thus if all the lives expired prior to twenty-one years of the lease agreement, then Wm. Hamilton's lease lasted twenty-one years. When this list was prepared two of the lives were dead and the minimum number of years were complete.
Source: Leslie estate papers (C.L.A., B2).

whether the same tenants will be continued on till November or be turned out and who would [he] wish to be continued there'. This illustrates the agent tracking the lives in the leases and re-illustrates Leslie's retention of control over tenant selection. When a lease did expire, it appears that Leslie had a preference to select a suitable tenant rather than auction the lease. The process of an auction of a lease would be inconsistent with Leslie's policy of choosing his tenants, illustrated earlier. Further, throughout the rent rolls, notes were recorded after holdings that needed to be valued, such as Wm. Smart's holding in Glaslough in the November 1803 rent roll.[63] Leslie's agents appear to have regularly visited the tenant's holdings, which allowed them to continuously track the value of the holdings. James McKenna of Killykeady was allowed 16*s.* 10*d.* off 'for want of measure' in 1823, as were James and Patrick McAtee, both of Killykeady, who were each allowed off £1 9*s.* 1*d.* 'for want of measure'.[64] Through his agents' work Leslie was always aware of the value of his land. From his agents' correspondence it is clear that tenants could not lease land without Leslie being satisfied with them. It is unlikely that he would have risked the lottery of an auction, which could result in a bad tenant.

The extant leases for the estates at Glaslough agreed during the life of Charles Powell Leslie II were generally of a standard printed form. John Diven's lease for his holding in the town of Glaslough was a typical lease, where he was required to pay '£7 sterling together with 6*d*. in the pound for every pound of the said reserved yearly rent, as receiver's fees' in two equal half yearly gale payments, on 1 May and 1 November.[65] John Diven did not pay a consideration or fine to enter the lease. None of the other extant leases contain a consideration or fine. Landlords who needed cash would look for an entry fine from the tenant and in return would offer the holding at a lower rent, thus sacrificing long term income for short term cash flow requirements. The absence of such a fine in Leslie's leases would indicate that he did not have cash flow or short term money difficulties, a view the buoyant rental incomes of the early nineteenth century supports. The renewal of the lease for the towns and lands of Skernageeragh (Emyvale) between Richard Benson and Christina Leslie and the trustees of the Leslie estates in 1834 was not on the standard printed form.[66] This was probably because it was a major contract and thus had terms and conditions which made the standard, printed, lease unsuitable. Like Diven's lease, this lease had no fine or consideration included, which indicates the sound financial state of these estates in the 1830s.

A middleman's lease from the Leslies imposed conditions on the subletting leases which were agreed with the undertenants. William Crookshanks, a merchant and a middleman, leased land at Drumturk to a number of undertenants, including Patrick Boyland, in the early nineteenth century. The lease between Crookshanks and Boyland made on 13 June 1795, for eleven acres, three roods and nine perches, was 'for and during the full and on expiration of the two first of the three lives contained in the grand land lease of the said premises, from Charles Powell Leslie esquire, to the said William Crookshanks.'[67] This illustrates how the terms and conditions in the undertenants' lease had to be within those agreed in the grand lease.

The leases provided Leslie with a forecast of his expected rental revenues from his landed estate investments. However in times of economic recession many tenants were unable to pay their rent leading to revenue shortfalls for Leslie. Throughout years of economic recession the Leslies still had to ensure their bills and debts were paid. For these reasons Leslie was very attentive to lost revenues and costs for his estates. He paid particular attention to the arrears during the post-war economic recession between 1816 and 1821, which is discussed in detail in the next chapter. Even in less depressed times Leslie always paid close attention to costs. At a parish vestry on 11 April 1803 Leslie objected to the cess valuation of the parish 'as unfair'.[68] The new valuation agreed in that year reduced the cess on Glaslough from £24 to £16.[69] His letters to John Fleming, his land steward for the demesne farm, also illustrates the attention he paid to managing the costs in his business:[70]

> John Fleming is to observe that Colonel Leslie looks to profit being made of the lands. Therefore he expects a considerable sum of money to be paid to Mr. Murdock – clear of labourers wages – and the wages and board wages given to John Fleming for managing the farm. There must be more attention paid to keep the labourer's bills down – or no profit can be had – if the wheat and other crops – such as potatoes and oats are not sold at a good price by this book – the profit will not pay the labourers bills – so Colonel Leslie loses the value of this land and John Fleming's wages.

The demesne farm was another source of income to the estate business. In addition the tillage farming referenced above, livestock was also raised on the farm. The livestock account kept by Fleming between November 1812 and August 1815 records the sale of bullocks for £1142 5*s.* 4½*d.* sheep for £398 19*s.* 11*d.* cows for £198 16*s.* 8½*d.* and horses for £131 3*s.* 7½*d.* showing the type of stock on the farm.[71] Using the prices paid by Fleming's predecessor, Charles Christianson, in 1811, this equates to approximately 199 sheep and eighty-one bullocks sold.[72]

As part of his land steward role Fleming hired local labour to work on the demesne farm. In the six days ending 5 December 1812, he used 109 man-days on the demesne farm.[73] The number of men employed varied each day, as did their tasks. Table 8 gives a list for two typical days. The presence of the Leslie family demesne at Glaslough provided an important boost to the local economy, both directly, through the payment of wages to staff and indirectly,

Table 8. Men employed on the Leslie demesne farm

Day	Number of men employed per task
Dec. 1 1812	• 3 taking up trees • 1 jobing at stables • 1 herd • 1 carpenter • 2 hedging • 1 slator • 1 attending do. • 6 planting trees • 7 trashing
Dec. 3 1812	• 1 herd • 1 carpenter • 1 slator • 1 attending do. • 1 jobing at stables • 15 at hay stack

Source: Leslie estate papers, vouchers (C.L.A., E3).

Table 9. Demesne farm payments

Date	Payment	£	s	d
1800				
Aug. 30	Thomas Hoy for making new road near the castle	23	14	½
1812				
Nov. 26	The dairymaid 4 weeks board wages	1	0	0
1813				
Feb. 6	Mr. McMaghn for a lock for the yard gate	0	4	10
April 26	John O'Neill blacksmith	6	10	2½
May 18	The groom for two mares	0	5	5
May 29	Jas. White for shearing 25 sheep	0	6	4
July 10	Wm. Whitsitt sadler	2	4	0
Aug. 7	John Carbery on account of turf cutting	2	0	0
1815				
Aug 1.	Andy Woods and John McKenna for weeding Clery ditches	1	2	9
1817				
Nov. 3	Repairs to office house at the castle	28	3	3½
1820				
Mar. 24	Wm. Johnston for newspapers	8	17	9

Source: Leslie estate papers, vouchers (C.L.A., E3), rentals (C.L.A., D1).

through payments to locals for services provided to the estate. Table 9 illustrates some typical payments.

In parallel to monitoring the costs in his estate business, Leslie took opportunities to increase his income when they occurred. He bought a number of estates during his life. One such estate was the small estate at Cordoo in the barony of Monaghan. Alexander Fleming carried out the valuation of this estate on 13 April 1815, which illustrates how estates were valued at that period – see table 10. The price recommended by Fleming to Leslie for the purchase of this estate was £3,074 0*s.* 4½*d.* This was lower than the true value, as the tenant's interest, which was related to the duration of the lives in the current lease would keep the rental income lower than the land could earn for nine years in Fleming's judgement. However, James Nixon investigated the two tenants and reported in his letter to Leslie on 21 April 1815, that Leslie 'might purchase both their interests on easy terms' due to their financial difficulties.[74] Thus, using the survey and Nixon's information, Leslie would be in position to make an early return on his investment. This analysis reveals that

Table 10. Valuation of the Cordoo estate by Alexander Fleming, 13 April 1815

Area: 125 Acres 1 roods 15 perches **Present yearly rent:** £34 8*s* 9*d*

- Leased to William Ley Esq. in 1760 for the lives of William Ley (now dead), Daniel Bradshaw (aged 77) and Beadal Bradshaw (aged 68), second and third sons of John Bradshaw of Lisabuck
- The undertenants of Mr. Ley offered last November to renew their leases with Mr. Coote at £2 10*s* per acre provided he would give them a lease of one life or twenty-one years.
- Fleming recommended that the land was worth 40*s*. per acre, yielding a yearly value of £250 13*s* 9*d* in 1815.

	£	*s*	*d*	
Present yearly value	250	13	9	• @ 40*s* per acre
Present yearly rent	34	5	5½	
Tenants yearly interest	215	8	3½	
@ 9 years purchase			x9	• Fleming's value on the remaining lives in the lease
Tenants Interest	**1,938**	**0**	**4½**	
Present yearly value	250	13	9	
@ 20 years purchase			x20	• Number of years purchase for return on investment
Gross Value	5,013	15	0	
Deduct Tenant Interest	1,938	0	4½	
Net Value	**3,074**	**0**	**4½**	• Exclusive of Turf bog

Source: Leslie estate papers (C.L.A., D4).

Leslie's return on capital employed was 5 per cent. This is higher than that expected by the marquis of Downshire from land purchases in County Down during the same period.[75] Perhaps this indicates that property investment in County Down was viewed as a better investment than property investment in County Monaghan. Or alternatively it may indicate that Charles Powell Leslie II expected or needed a better return on his investment.

The above analysis also placed a value on the tenant's interest because of the lease held. Although there is no explicit mention of tenant right in the estate records or other sources for the parish of Donagh during these years, it is probable that it existed and was respected, as it was prevalent in the neighbouring parishes in Ulster. The Devon commission, which studied tenant right as part of its investigations, unfortunately neither visited Donagh nor interviewed anyone from Donagh. However, it interviewed individuals from neighbouring parishes, where tenant right was recorded as being present and respected, such as on the Caledon estate in County Tyrone, the Leslies' neighbours, and in neighbouring County Monaghan parishes, such as Tedavnet.[76]

Another opportunity for Leslie to increase his income arose in 1816 when the Monaghan militia was disbanded and only a permanent staff of four officers and ninety-one men were retained.[77] Leslie, their colonel, ordered them to Glaslough town, where they were to remain until further orders. Twelve of them took holdings in the Demesne, in 1818, for a half-yearly rent of over £76.[78]

Leslie provided patronage to his friends of the staff. In 1822 when the number of men on the Monaghan staff was reduced to fifty-five. Leslie found positions in the newly established police force of Ireland for those not entitled to a pension.[79] In fact most were promoted at once to the rank of sergeant. In 1828 when the staff were again reduced in number, Leslie again took care of those not retained on the staff. He arranged the appointment of two staff members as county and assistant surveyors, while another was appointed governor of the County Louth prison at Dundalk.[80] Leslie's friends also had county appointments, Nixon was sheriff in 1815.[81] As stated earlier some of his agents were members of the grand jury. This patronage and local political activity could be used by Leslie to aid his business.

While Leslie gave patronage to his friends he also looked for patronage from the government for himself. In October 1811 he wrote to his relative Richard Ryder, home secretary, asking him to obtain the bishopric of Dromore for Leslie's brother John, dean of Cork.[82] Ultimately, he hoped to get his brother appointed bishop of Clogher because of the influence this appointment had over some of the Leslies estates. On 21 May 1807 he wrote to his cousin Sir Arthur Wellesley, lord lieutenant, requesting to be appointed as a trustee to the linen board, an appointment he took up in the same year.[83]

Leslie's approach to politics was more as an extension to his business interests than based on political ambition for its own end. As an M.P. he had influence and a vote in the house of parliament giving him leverage with the government, which he usually supported, allowing him to look for patronage for himself, his friends and his constituents in return.[84] Following Leslie's defeat in the 1826 election by Henry Westenra, who had the support of the Catholic Association, his friends wrote to him referring to this Catholic victory as 'a deep and deadly blow at the independence of the county . . . [it has] thrown its whole representation into the hands of the Roman Catholic clergy'.[85] Leslie responded 'The tie between landlord and tenant has been dissolved, and the gentry and landed proprietors, have been totally bereft of their political influence, and as you gentlemen properly observe the entire representation has been thrown into the hands of the Roman Catholic clergy'.[86] In a later letter in December 1826 Leslie thanked his supporters and felt confident they would 'uphold what the state of your country, as well as that of the empire demands, The Protestant ascendancy in church and state.'[87]

This correspondence clearly shows Leslie and his supporters in opposition to Catholic emancipation. Catholic emancipation would remove political power from their control and thus damage their independence. However, the independence referred to was that of the Protestant ascendancy. Loss of political power diminished Leslie's influence and his ability to utilise patronage to benefit his landed estates business. Thus his anti-Catholic stance cannot be viewed as simple sectarianism, it had a business perspective.

Charles Powell Leslie II's management of his estates demonstrated many of the attributes which Kerby Miller associated with early nineteenth century landlord's responses to the economic changing times. Leslie was active in his estate management, maintaining control through his agents, to whom he delegated only limited authority. Charles Powell Leslie II was a typical landed businessman, carefully monitoring expenditure, expecting profits and seizing opportunities to grow his business. He established direct relationships with his tenants by reducing the number of middlemen on his estates and through maintaining control of tenant selection himself. He also reduced the number of leases. However, he did not eliminate middlemen and leases completely as they were both still evident on the estates after his death. His politics were in many ways an extension of his business needs whose future he believed was best served by the Protestant ascendancy in church and state.

The estate and its community in changing times

Population growth was one of the most significant changes in Irish society between the Act of Union and the Famine. This increase took place in a period of economic change, which went from boom to bust. The population in Ireland had been increasing from the second half of the eighteenth century. The domestic linen industry both permitted and required these levels of population growth in terms of increased density of population and flexible household membership.[1] Thus this industry was a contributor to the population growth. The 1821 census put Ireland's population at 6,801,827. This increased to 8,175,124 in the 1841 census.[2] However, as table 11 illustrates, this rate of population increase did not happen in the parish of Donagh.

Table 11. 1821, 1831, and 1841 census returns summary for the parish of Donagh, County Monaghan

Parish or Town	1821		1831			1841		
	No. of Persons	% of Parish	No. of Persons	% of Parish	% change since 1821	No. of Persons	% of Parish	% change since 1821
Donagh P.	10,467	100	11,068	100	+5.7	10,244	100	-2.1
Emyvale T.	535	5.1	571	5.2	+6.7	694	6.8	+29.7
Glasslough T.	847	8.1	812	7.3	−4.1	562	5.5	−33.6

Source: Census of Ireland 1821, 1831 and 1841.

The table shows that the majority of the community in Donagh lived outside the towns of Glaslough and Emyvale. The population in the parish rose gradually between 1821 and 1831 and then dropped during the 1830s. This trend may reflect the impact of the well-documented emigration from the parish of Donagh during the 1830s.[3] The population in the neighbouring parishes of Errigal Trough, Monaghan and Tedavnet all increased during this period, while the parish of Tehallan, south of Donagh, experienced a pattern of population change similar to Donagh. In 1813 William Shaw Mason's *Statistical account of Ireland* recorded the population of the barony of Trough, which consisted of the two parishes Donagh and Errigal Trough, as 15,230, compared with the census figure in 1821 of 17,974, indicating Donagh's population was probably increasing prior to 1821.[4] Within the parish of

Donagh, the town of Glaslough experienced continuous population decline, while the neighbouring town of Emyvale experienced continuous population growth, and if the figures in the census reports are taken as accurate, significant growth between 1831 and 1841. By 1841, Emyvale's population had surpassed the population of Glaslough. By analysing the parish registers for the Church of Ireland community and the Presbyterian community a better understanding of these population changes can be gained.

A general trend in the number of Church of Ireland marriages at Glaslough can be detected by subdividing this span of forty-years into four ten year periods and calculating the mean number of marriages for each period, see table 12. This approach shows that the number of marriages was decreasing. The mean number of marriages for the years 1832–41 was nearly half the mean number of marriages between 1802 and 1811.

Table 12. Number of Church of Ireland marriages per ten-year period

Years	No. of marriages	Mean no. of marriages per annum	Standard deviation from mean
1802–11	111	11.1	5.8
1812–21	84	8.4	3.0
1822–31	63	7.0	2.2
1832–41	58	5.8	3.3

Source: Donagh Parish registers, 1796–1841 (D.P.R.1(a), 1(b), 2 & 3).

Analysis of the baptismal registers for the Church of Ireland parish of Donagh provides an insight into the number of births within this community. Table 13 summarises the number of Church of Ireland baptisms registered in the forty-year period. The mean number of baptisms per annum for each ten-year period indicates that the number of baptisms decreased by approximately fifty percent between 1802 and 1841.

Table 13. Number of Church of Ireland baptisms per ten-year period

Years	No. of Baptism	Emyvale		Glaslough		Mean no. of baptisms per annum	Standard deviation from mean
		No. of baptism	Percentage of total	No. of baptism	Percentage of total		
1802–11	612	45	7.4	97	15.8	61.2	10.0
1812–21	525	32	6.1	80	15.2	52.5	7.2
1822–31	475	44	9.3	70	14.7	47.5	10.6
1832–41	315	23	7.3	58	18.4	31.5	6.8

Source: Donagh Parish registers, 1796–1841 (D.P.R.1(a), 1(b), 2 & 3).

Table 14. Age distribution at death, for males and females, recorded in the Church of Ireland parish of Donagh's burial registers, 1802–41

Years	Percentage of those buried who died before 40 years old			Percentage of those buried who died before 60 years old		
	Male	Female	Total	Male	Female	Total
1802–11	34.8	39.1	36.8	67.0	71.7	69.2
1812–21	30.1	33.3	32.0	51.2	53.3	52.3
1822–31	40.8	28.4	34.6	63.4	48.4	55.9
1832–41	35.5	29.4	32.3	56.6	41.2	48.4

Source: Donagh Parish registers, 1796–1841 (D.P.R.1(a), 1(b), 2 & 3).

Analysis of the age of those buried as recorded in the Church of Ireland registers reveals the life expectancy of the parishioners – see table 14. This analysis illustrates that there was an increase in the life expectancy amongst the women of the Church of Ireland community. Between 1802 and 1811, 39.1 per cent of the parish's Church of Ireland women buried had died before they reached the age of forty, whereas between 1832 and 1841, only 29.4 per cent of the women buried had died before they reached the age of forty. Declining childbirth, which would be indicated by the decreases in marriages and baptisms, may have been a contributing reason for more women living beyond forty years, as the number of women dying in childbirth would have decreased. Another possible contribution to the increased life expectancy of women in the parish may have been emigration of the parish's younger generation, leaving only the older generation's burials to be recorded in the registers. However, this does not explain why this was only a female phenomena as the analysis does not allow the same significant conclusions to be drawn regarding men's life expectancy in the parish, where no consistent change can be observed.

The analysis of the Church of Ireland registers shows that births and marriages within this community were in decline between 1802 and 1841. Yet the number of baptisms always exceeded the number of burials. Table 15 shows the ratio of burials to baptisms for each 10-year period. These figures show that there were approximately twice as many baptisms as burials, though this ratio decreased overtime.

Table 15. Ratio of Church of Ireland burials to baptisms for each 10-year period

Years	1802–1811	1812–21	1822–31	1832–41
Baptisms	612	525	475	315
Burials	224	248	199	165
Ratio baptisms/burials	2.7	2.1	2.4	1.9

Source: Donagh Parish registers, 1796–1841 (D.P.R.1(a), 1(b), 2 & 3).

With increased life expectancy and the number of baptisms consistently exceeding the number of burials, one would expect the population of the Church of Ireland community to have increased over the forty year period. However, this is inconsistent with the census returns for 1821, 1831 and 1841 for the town of Glaslough, the centre of the Church of Ireland community, which recorded continuous decline. If the census figures are taken as accurate then part of this community in Donagh had to be migrating from the parish as otherwise the population would have increased. The Church of Ireland Protestants who generally differed in occupation, custom and wealth from their Catholic neighbours viewed marriage and the provision for a family as a serious undertaking desiring to acquire wealth and competence for its support.[5] The general economic decline during these years would probably trigger the decrease in marriages and baptisms in this community as prospective husbands found it more difficult to provide security for a family unit, thus altering when they got married or encouraging them to leave the locality. Miller's *Emigrants and exiles* has shown that the initial emigrants from nineteenth-century Ireland were predominantly Protestants from Ulster.[6] These initial emigrants were primarily middle class with sufficient wealth to pay the high fairs to Canada and the Unitied States of America. It was not until the 1830s that Catholic emigration exceeded Protestant emigration as the cost of passage fairs dropped, however, Ulster's Protestants continued to emigrate in significant numbers. The Church of Ireland community in the parish of Donagh were typical candidates for this initial wave of emigrants.

The marriage and baptismal registers for the Presbyterian community at Glennan, although not as complete, allows comparisons to be made between the different communities. Unfortunately, the marriage records only cover the years 1805–20. Prior to 1810 there were less than ten marriages per year, whereas in the subsequent ten years the number of marriages was always in excess of ten per annum and exceeded twenty per annum on five occasions, with a peak of twenty-eight marriages in 1815. The evidence appears to indicate that marriages were increasing in this community however, the span of years is too short for this to be stated conclusively.[7] The register of baptisms at Glennan is more complete covering the years from 1805 to 1841. The summary in table 16, reveals a different trend to that recorded in the Church of Ireland baptism registers. The mean number of baptisms per annum for each ten-year period indicates that the number of baptisms decreased gradually up to 1831 before increasing rapidly in the 1830s, peaking at sixty-seven baptisms in 1835, and exceeding the number of Church of Ireland baptisms over the same span of years indicating a growing community.

During the period 1821 to 1841 the population of the civil parish of Donagh remained reasonably constant. The above analysis of the baptismal, marriage and burial registers indicates that the Presbyterian community was growing and there is circumstantial evidence of a gradual decline in the

Table 16. Number of Presbyterian baptisms per period

Years	No. of baptism	Mean no. of baptisms per annum	Standard deviation from mean
1805–11*	295	42.1	10.5
1812–21	412	41.2	6.9
1822–31	376	37.6	7.4
1832–41	484	48.4	9.5

* *Note*: The first period 1805–11 does not represent a full ten-year period.
Source: Baptisms of Glennan Presbyterian church, 1805–41 (P.R.O.N.I., MIC 1P/155/1).

Church of Ireland community, possibly due to emigration. This view is supported by the 1834 report of the commissioners of public instruction, which noted that the average attendance at Glaslough church was 250 and had been stationary for the previous five years. Similarly the small Methodist community in the parish had an average attendance of forty and this also had been stationary for the previous five years. While the Presbyterian meeting house had an average attendance of 500 which was increasing and the two Catholic chapels in the parish, at Corracrin and Glennan, had attendances of 840 and 1,204 respectively which were also increasing.[8] The trigger for the decrease in baptisms and marriages in the Church of Ireland community is unclear. It appears to have started before rather than after the post war recession. It may have been the changes in the linen industry, decline in the role of middlemen, the growth in radicalism in the late eighteenth century or new opportunities in other parts of Ireland or the British empire for a community closest to the British establishment. However, once the economic recession set-in, as Miller commented, for these Protestants 'emigration was not exile but opportunity or at worst escape'.[9]

The post-war economic recession brought major financial difficulties to the Leslies and the community living on their estates. This recession was further exacerbated by the famine of 1817. Figure 7 shows the arrears on the Leslie estates near Glaslough between 1800 and 1840. By 1816 the arrears on the Glaslough and Emyvale estates equated to over 50 per cent of their rental income illustrating the depth of this economic recession in the locality and its impact on the Leslies' income.[10] The cumulative arrears for the Leslie estates near Glaslough peaked at £3,212 in 1816, just two years after the end of the war in Europe.

The tenants on the small Hutcheson estate near Glaslough were generally always able to pay their rents, thus no arrears were recorded. It is probable that these tenants had leases with a relatively low rent, which could easily be paid. This view that the Hutcheson estate had leases, which were favourable to the tenant is supported by Leslie's desire to buy these leases, which is indicated in

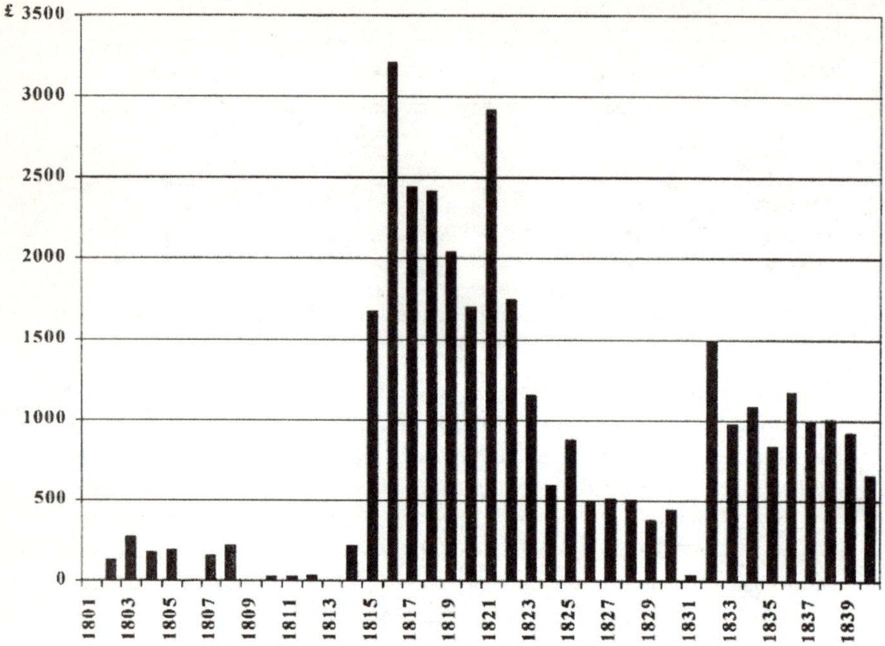

7. Arrears on the Leslie estates at Glaslough, 1801–40
Source: C.L.A., D1, D1A; N.L.I., Ms 5813

a letter from James Nixon to Charles Powell Leslie II in November 1823, when he wrote 'I shall write to G . . . about the leases of the Hutcheson lands, but he stated before that he thought it impossible to procure them'.[11] The impact of the recession on the local community is recorded in the rent rolls of 1816–17 by the increased references to tenants in arrears and 'out of possession'.[12] However, not all the tenants who fell into arrears were required or decided to give up their holdings. Andrew McGee who had arrears of £22 16*s.* 11½*d.* on a holding in Tully with a half yearly rent of £8 10*s.* 4½*d.* continued in possession as did James Corly and Patrick Treanor in the same townland. These three tenants all managed to pay some of their rent in the half year ending 1 November 1817, though these amounts were less than was due for the half year. Patrick McAtee and William Kelly both with holdings in Killykeady for £6 7*s.* 1*d.* per half year, each had arrears of over £19 and paid no rent in the half year ending November 1817, yet they retained possession. The explanation of how some tenants retained their holdings whereas others went out of possession possibly lies in their ability to pay the arrears sometime in the future. Generally, those out of possession had arrears significantly in excess of their half yearly rent. Hugh Lavery with arrears of £47 1*s.* 5*d.* in November 1817 on his holding in Mullan, which had a half yearly rent of £7 10*s.* was recorded as out of possession. However, there was no standard rule, as

Alexander Armstrong with a holding in Tullyree at a half-yearly rental of £3. 8*s.* 3*d.* had outstanding arrears of £19. 9*s.* 6*d.* in the same year and paid no rent for that half year, yet he retained his holding.

The total arrears for November 1819 were in excess of £1,900, on 193 holdings.[13] This was a huge crisis in the community. There were too many tenants in arrears for individuals to be seen as in default. Further, those in arrears included prominent locals like Leslie's friend Captain Ross for his holding in Glaslough.[14] James Nixon writing to Leslie in June 1817 referring to meeting Leslie in Glaslough wrote 'your presence never was more wanting, the greatest distress present in the country and amongst many people far above the lowest order'.[15] The total arrears lost between 1816 and 1821 on the Glaslough, Emyvale and Montgomery estates was £1,725. 15*s.* 4½*d.*[16]

Leslie's approach to this crisis was to actively manage the arrears situation. He had separate accounts made, to track the arrears on the estate thus allowing them to be identified clearly and viewed separately from the main estate accounts.[17] Leslie and his agents viewed good tenants as an asset to the business of a landed estate and thus desirable to be retained even during economic difficulties. This is illustrated in a letter from James Nixon during the later crisis in the 1830s from Pettigoe where he wrote 'I could not get a farthing more without destroying your tenants and injuring your property'.[18] In another letter Nixon expressed the importance of getting good tenants 'I think for so far, I have succeeded in getting a better description of tenants'.[19] The rent rolls record that Leslie was not detached and uncompromising regarding his tenants' difficulties. Denis McCarole and Peter McCabe, both on the Montgomery estate, with arrears of £10. 7*s.* 6½*d.* and £6. 4*s.* 10*d.* respectively, were allowed off their arrears in 1819.[20] Mrs. Leslie also forgave tenants their arrears in later economically depressed times. John Heatley who held land in Drumbanagher with an annual rent of £4. 10*s.* had accumulated arrears of £7. 11*s.* 6*d.* in 1840, which Mrs Leslie forgave.[21] Peter McGeagh of Glaslough and Thomas Woods of Mullanlary were also forgiven their arrears in 1840.[22] James and Catherine McKenna of Tavanagh had their arrear forgiven and rent reduced 'on account of road damage'.[23]

In general a landlord had a number of options to recover arrears for non-payment of rent:[24] through seizure of the tenant's goods; or, by use of court process. After two government acts in 1816 and 1820 a civil bill of ejectment could be obtained in the case where the tenant had a lease with an annual rent of £50 or less. A civil bill of ejectment could not be used where the tenant had a lease of more than £50. The legal costs of ejecting such a tenant could be significant. However, for a landlord to obtain a civil bill of ejectment, he had to prove the tenant owed half a year's rent, the premises had been deserted and there was insufficient crop and stock to meet the rent by distraint, or that the tenant owed a full year's rent. Where the tenant had no lease it was necessary to serve him notice to quit and then proceed against him using the same civil bill legal process. The tenant was treated as one whose legal interest had been determined but who was still in possession. Thus the tenant had legal rights and could defend himself in court and frequently such a defence was successful.[25]

Leslie's policy regarding how his agents handled the recovery of arrears appears to have been mixed. In 1803 Leslie's agents had seized the cattle of John Wilson of Cornacrieve for an arrear of £4. 12*s.* 3*d.*, his half yearly rent.[26] Peter Callaghan of Tiramoan had his goods seized for his arrears of a half years rent of £1. 15*s.* in the same year. However, neither tenant was ejected from their holdings, as they continued to pay their rents in later years.[27] Legal process was also resorted to. Leslie's account, of December 1806, with his solicitor, Mitchell, includes the costs of £40. 7*s.* 6*d.* for an ejectment brought against Mr. Benson for non-payment of rent.[28] In April 1810 Robert Murdock, Leslie's agent, issued the following notice to quit to Hugh Holland, Owen McKenna, James Kelly, Pat Kelly, John Kelly, Pat Raferty and all others concerned:[29]

> Take notice that I hereby require you to deliver up to Charles Powell Leslie Esqr on his order on the first day of November next the quiet and peaceable possession of that part of the lands of Corlattallen now in your possession otherwise he will proceed against you for recovery of the possession thereof according to law given under my hand this 21st day of April 1810.

However, very few if any of these tenants appear to have been ejected and Pat Raferty, Owen McKenna, John Kelly and Pat Kelly still had their holdings in Corlattallen in the 1830s.[30] During the post war recession Leslie appears to have taken a flexible approach, aware that mass ejectments was of little long-term value to him or his business. However, some tenants were ejected for non-payment of rent. In a letter to Leslie from Pettigo in October 1823, James Nixon recalled the ejectment of John Muldoon, 'a very troublesome man' whom in 1821 he had sent 'to Lifford Jail for the costs of an ejectment decree'.[31] Nixon continued 'he is totally unable to pay and now sufficiently punished perhaps you would think it right to permit me discharge him'.

The Leslies' agents had a key role to track tenants' ability to pay their rents and arrears. The agents were expected to visit tenants regularly and observe whether the tenant was likely to have difficulty in paying their rents. A letter from Robert Murdock to Leslie in May 1819 illustrates this activity where he wrote regarding some tenants, 'as they are cropping these lands there is no danger of these rents.'[32] An undated lease book from the 1840s provides further evidence of this type of report. The agent recorded 'James Brown, Tully, is cropping his land says he will soon pay his rent'.[33] For James Corly of Tully the agent recorded 'he can't crop his land nor pay his rent I told him to be in on Friday'. While 'Owen McKenna is cropping his land can't pay rent for some time.' For John Douglas of Killyrean the agent wrote 'no means of cropping his land, Douglas in poor house'. Thus the agent's judgement was relied on by the Leslies to assess the tenants ability to pay the rent or whether legal process would be invoked. The approach adopted was the one most likely to continue to provide ongoing revenues to the landlord.

The severity of the post-war recession on the local community was also recorded in the Church of Ireland vestry minutes. The first reference to the poor in the community was in the vestry minutes of 15 April 1816, where a sum of £2 was given to 'Margaret Newell, a pauper'.[34] The continuing recession in the community was recorded in the following year's minutes of 7 April 1817 where a further sum of £7 was levied on the parish for Margaret Newell and Mary Woods.[35] By August 1817 the impact of the famine required a sum of £20 to be levied on the parish 'to purchase coffins for the poor' in addition to £20 levied earlier in the year.[36] These hard times continued in the parish the following year, where the vestry raised £5 for 'coffins for said poor' and continued to provide support for the poor in the community including Margaret Newell and Ellen Woods.[37] The Presbyterian baptism registers also provide evidence of members of the community falling on hard times. On 3 April 1820, the minister recorded the baptism of John M'Cracken whom he refers to as the child of a 'beggar woman', whose husband was William M'Cracken.[38] As the local economy declined people left the parish. Bernard Callaghan who held land in the townlands of Mullaghduff and Billis was recorded as having left the country in the Leslie rent rolls of September 1819.[39]

The famine of 1817 had a severe impact in this parish. The Church of Ireland burial registers, which provide an indicator of the good and sickly years within the community recorded the highest number of deaths in 1817.[40] The forty-nine deaths in this year exceed the next worst year, 1812, by twelve deaths, while the mean over the forty years covered by the registers was twenty-one per annum. Following the failure of the potato crop in 1816, 1817 was a year of harsh famine and its impact is reflected in the registers. By the summer of 1817, fever was general. In Monaghan few households of the poorer community escaped.[41] Although the years 1802–16 were famine free, there were other famines between 1817 and 1841, for example 1821. The burial registers record twenty-three deaths in 1821, which was not an excessive number of deaths. There were many years when this number of burials was exceeded. The difference between 1817 and other famine years was the severity of the famine and the fact it was accompanied by an outbreak of typhus.[42] The wealth of the generally better-off Church of Ireland community could sustain them in lean years so that normally they were unaffected by famine, unlike their poorer neighbours. However, from the registers it appears that in years where the famine was accompanied by diseases such as typhus, no group, rich, middle-class or poor could insulate themselves from its impact. In the parish of Donagh, twenty-eight of the forty-nine burials were females in 1817.[43]

During this epidemic, the dispensary doctor from the Strabane area recorded that nearly two-thirds of the dispensary patients were female, a fact he attributed to the amount of time women spent indoors and nursing the sick.[44] The same probably applied to the women parishioners of Donagh. Richard Moffat the surgeon of the Glaslough and Emyvale dispensary in his report for 1837–8 referred to this problem of friends being required 'to associate constantly with individuals' who were sick as it was necessary to treat the fever cases at their homes.[45]

Although some sort of economic stability was restored in the 1820s on north County Monaghan estates as evidenced by the rental income and arrears for the Leslie estates at Glaslough. The economy deteriorated in the 1830s, arrears once again increasing. Captain Ross, agent for some of Leslie's north Monaghan estates, reported to Mrs Leslie in July 1831, 'I am now doing everything to get the rent from those tenants who disobliged the colonel, they are very poor and it will not be easily got'.[46] James Nixon wrote from Glaslough in April 1831, also reporting on the economic decline, 'I never saw so much poverty in this country or so much difficulty in getting rents collected'.[47] The evidence provided in the poor inquiry of the 1830s provides an insight into the lives of the poor in the parish of Donagh who suffered most in these economic depressed times. These poor were not a homogenous group and had different arrangements for earning their living. Some were cottier-weavers dependent on farmers for a small piece of land, a cabin and supplies of yarn, others were subtenants to a farmer who supplied them with a handloom at which the cottier's family worked for the benefit of its dwarf landlord, more precarious than these was the landless householder who had only a 'dry cot', that is, a cabin without land.[48]

Thomas Johnston reported to the inquiry that these poor agricultural labourers held their property from both head landlords and middlemen.[49] The Catholic parish priest, Father Moynagh, referred to the labourers' landlords as the middle-class.[50] Their holdings were seldom let without land, usually a rood or a half rood of land. Their rent varied depending on the nature of their holding, from £3. 12*s.* for a holding of one rood, a house or cabin and bog to £2. 2*s.* for a cabin with a half rood of land and no bog, while those who held a cabin with no land paid 6*d.* per week.[51] The tenants rent did not usually include any duty labour, though landlords called for some days in spring and harvest. Father Moynagh described their cabins as 'very bad, sod walls or stones, without lime mortar. For the greater part without bedding, and very frequently no bedsteads.'[52] James Hoy, surgeon at the Glaslough and Emyvale dispensary stated 'In visiting the poor I have found at least two-thirds of them in a state of misery and distress and more than one-third are strangers to the necessary comforts of life, unless supplied by some charitable person.'[53] Thomas Johnston responding to the questions regarding the number of labourers in the parish stated that since 'the great depression in the linen trade, the great body of weavers in the parish, which are about one half of the population, have become labourers *pro tempore* . . . I cannot say the number in full or occasional employment, they so vary from the above cause.'[54] When out of employment the labourers survived on the potatoes of their conacres.[55] The winter-time was when these labourers were least employed. While the harvest and the spring were the times when they were most likely to be employed.[56] Their wages varied from 6*d.* per day including diet or 10*d.* per day without diet in the summer to 6*d* per day without diet in winter.[57] Women and children were usually only employed as agricultural labourers for a few weeks at the harvest and spring at 3*d.* to 5*d.* per day without diet.[58] The labourer's wages were paid in either money, provisions or con acre, or a combination of these. These labourers relied on employment in tillage farming as Donagh was not a grazing parish and so did not provide employment with herds.[59] Father Moynagh estimated that 90 per cent of the land in the parish was arable and that only one-fifth of this arable land was under pasture, emphasising the dominance of tillage in the parish.[60] Conacre, which was eagerly sought, was viewed by Johnston, Pratt and Moynagh as providing a remunerating crop, which 'poor men without land, could not otherwise support them and their families' according to Moynagh.[61] Johnston added that 'no excessive rents charged for con acre in this parish.'[62]

Father Moynagh stated that the ordinary diet of the labourer and his family was potatoes and during the summer months they also would have some buttermilk.[63] James Hoy, surgeon, expressed the view that the reliance on the potato 'particularly in the months of August and September, promotive of disease, diarrhoea particularly.'[64] He stated that he had found many instances where disease had been brought on by unwholesome food.

The reports from the Glaslough and Emyvale dispensary provide an insight into the nature of the illnesses and their causes in the community. It had been established in 1818 to supply 'the poor with medicine and medical attention'.[65] It was supported by grand jury presentments and private contributions. The list of subscribers in 1837 included Mrs Leslie with largest contribution of £20.[66] Other contributors included William Anketell, £15; William Murdock, £2. 2*s*; Thomas Johnston, £1. 1*s*.; Reverand W.H. Pratt, £1. 1*s*.; Robert Murdock, £1. 1*s.* and Father Moynagh £1. 1*s.* The rules of the dispensary stated that 'tenants of those land proprietors who have not subscribed to the funds of the dispensary shall not be entitled to medical advice for attendance from the dispensary,' thus obligating landlords to support the dispensary.[67] The surgeon attended the dispensary between ten o'clock and two o'clock on Tuesdays and Fridays at Glaslough and Mondays and Thursdays at Emyvale.[68] The surgeon also attended those sick who were unable to attend the dispensary.[69] Richard Moffet, surgeon, reported for the year 1836–7:[70]

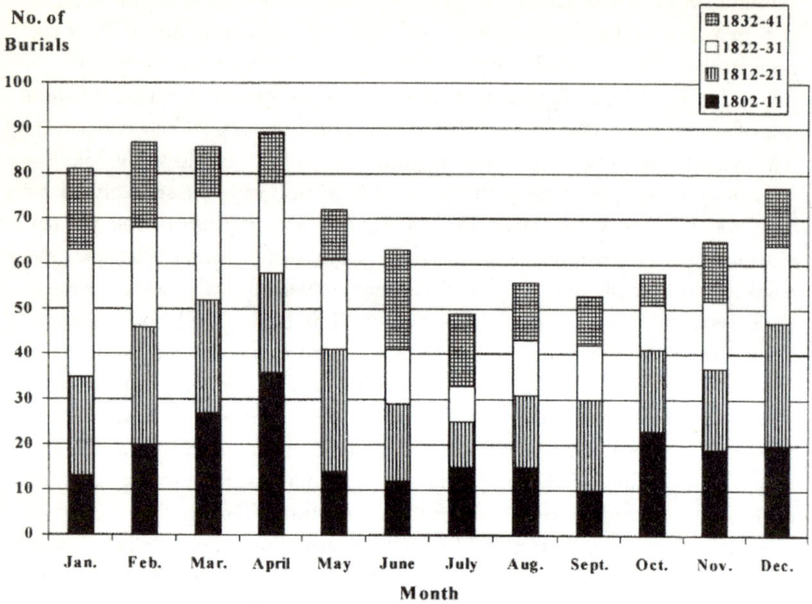

8. Monthly burials in Donagh's Church of Ireland parish register, 1802–41

> the majority of instances the fever of this district was typhoid, and its progress in many families was of the most afflicting nature, from 3 to 6 being frequently ill at the same time. This melancholy fact is chiefly attributable to: the destitute state of the people; the want of proper clothing and nourishment calculated to sustaining friends of the patients in their incumbent duties at the bedside.

For the year 1837–8, he reported that there had been a significant decrease in the number of smallpox cases, primarily because the people had ensured that their children were vaccinated, which had not been the case in 1836–7, when seventy cases of smallpox had occurred.[71] However, the number of cases of fever had not only increased, but was also of a more formidable nature than in previous years, even though the alleged causes for the outbreak in 1836 had not been in force to the same extent in the winter of 1837, fuel having been more abundant and the articles of diet cheaper.[72] The seasons of winter and spring were those when deaths occurred most frequently amongst the Donagh population as is shown in figure 8.

The declining living conditions of the poorer classes is further emphasised in the poor inquiry. Thomas Johnston's view was that the conditions of the poorer classes had deteriorated since 1815 because of 'the want of prosperity in the linen trade' and an increasing population.[73] Father Moynagh stated that the clothing of the labouring classes was the coarsest and cheapest kind and frequently patched for many years.[74] Despite the declining living conditions, the parish of Donagh remained generally undisturbed in the 1830s. Father Moynagh remarked it was 'always peaceable', a comment echoed by the vicar, Reverend Pratt, who stated 'we live in peace and harmony here'.[75] These sentiments were also expressed by Leslie's agent, Robert Murdock, in his letter to Leslie in October 1831, where he remarked 'This country is very quiet at present I never saw it more so.'[76] However, Thomas Johnston remarked that there were occasional disturbances in his response to the poor inquiry.[77] This is not surprising considering the depressed economic times, but from the remarks of Murdock, Pratt and Moynagh, it appears disturbances were infrequent.

The economic recession and associated famine of 1817 triggered a new era of emigration from Ireland in numbers far in excess of anything seen before.[78] This emigration was still continuing in the 1830s. Father Moynagh, in his response to the poor inquiry, estimated that there were about fifty emigrants per year of the middle class leaving the parish for north America.[79] The vicar, Reverend Pratt, also held the view that the emigrants were 'two or three degrees above paupers'.[80] Whole families emigrated. In March 1839, Charlotte Wilson aged eleven years, daughter of William and Jane Wilson of Tonihamigan, was baptised in the Protestant parish church at Glaslough, prior to their emigration to America.[81] Thomas Johnston also commented that there had been 'a great number' of emigrants.[82] All those interviewed by the poor inquiry remarked that the emigrants received no assistance for the purpose of emigration from the parish of Donagh.[83] As discussed earlier many of these emigrants were probably Protestants, however, large numbers of Catholics from the parish of Donagh also emigrated to Prince Edward Island, Canada.[84] The impact of the initial emigration was probably to reduce the wealthier middle class in the parish's society, which were primarily Protestant, thus weakening the Protestant ascendancy. The Protestant community in Donagh because of its significant size was probably not as severely affected by this development as other parishes in Ireland, where those who remained behind became more isolated amongst their more populous Catholic neighbours whose influence grew with each passing year of the nineteenth century.

During the booming economy of the late eighteenth century and early nineteenth century, subdivision of holdings between family members had in general reduced the size of tenants' holdings in Ireland. However, with the declining economy after 1815, very small holdings were unable to support a family. Some landlords started to consolidate small holdings and the practice of impartible inheritance became more prevalent amongst tenant farmers.[85] Both of these actions reversed the earlier trend of subdivision and increased or maintained the size of holdings. Unfortunately, there is no extant early nineteenth-century survey of the Leslie estates near Glaslough detailing the size of tenants' holdings. However, using the tithe applotment books, the Leslie rent rolls for 1833 and a 1765 estate survey, the size of the holdings that tenants leased can be analysed for some townlands on the Leslie estates. Table 17 shows that these holdings were predominately between three and ten Irish plantation acres in 1833. This corresponds to approximately five to fifteen statute acres.[86]

Table 17. Size of holdings in the townlands of Drumcaw, Derrylea and Tiramoan in the parish of Donagh, County Monaghan, 1833

Townland	Number of holdings	10 acres +, Irish plantation measure	From 3 to 10 acres Irish plantation measure	< 3 acres Irish plantation measure
Drumcaw	14	7	7	0
Derrylea	13	1	10	2
Tiramoan	8	1	5	2
Total	**35**	**9**	**22**	**4**
Percentage	–	25.7	62.9	11.4

Source: Tithe applotment book (N.A.I., T.A.B. 23/2); Leslie estate papers rentals (C.L.A., D1A).

The largest holding in these townlands, at nineteen acres, was in Drumcaw. The townlands of Derrylea and Tiramoan had one holding of twelve acres and sixteen acres, respectively, while all their other holdings were six acres or less. Thus the majority of the holdings were less than ten Irish plantation acres. This corresponds with Father Moynagh's response to the poor inquiry, when he described the holdings as being between six and ten acres, held from the head landlord.[87] Thomas Johnston stated that 'the inhabitants being principally weavers, the farms are only from one acre to ten acres each, except in a very few instances, in which there are twenty to thirty acre farms.[88] Reverend Pratt's view was that the farms were 'two, four or six acres' held from the head landlord.[89] The marquis of Downshire, a progressive landlord in the early nineteenth century, regarded fifteen acres as the minimum desirable.[90]

The landless labourers were not recorded in the rent rolls or the tithe applotment books. The 1831 census recorded 595 males who were not occupiers employed as agricultural labourers in the rural parts of Donagh.[91] This represented approximately 26 per cent of the male population of twenty years or older. Based on an average household size in Monaghan of 5.2 persons, the landless population can be calculated for the Leslie townlands of Drumcaw, Derrylea and Tiramoan in 1841. This calculation is shown in table 18, confirming their presence and their percentage of the townland's population, which is similar to the parish calculation. The addition of these landless labourers and their families on these townlands increased the population endeavouring to live off small holdings.

Table 18. Landless population in Drumcaw, Derrylea and Tiramoan in the parish of Donagh, County Monaghan 1841

Townland	No. of holdings	Population of tenants with holdings	1841 population	Landless Number	Landless Percentage
Drumcaw	14	73	102	29	28
Derrylea	13	68	95	27	28
Tiramoan	8	42	63	21	33

Source: *Census of Ireland 1851;* Leslie estate papers rentals (N.L.I., Ms. 5813).

In 1841, Donagh was one of the more densely populated parishes in County Monaghan, which, as Freeman has illustrated, contained some of the most heavily populated rural areas in Ireland.[92] Monaghan had similar population pressures to the west of Ireland. The average rural population density in the county was fifty-eight persons per 100 acres (370 persons per square mile).[93] However, one quarter of the townlands in Monaghan had population densities of more than seventy-six persons per 100 acres.[94] Some of the townlands in Donagh had population densities at these levels, though none reached the densities of 1,300 persons per square mile of the baronies of Dartrey and Farney.[95] Table 19 shows the distribution of population densities on the rural townlands in Donagh. 29 per cent of townlands in the parish had more than seventy-six persons per 100 acres, higher than the county average. However, the townlands on the Leslie estates were not as densely populated. Only 17 per cent of the townlands on the Leslie estate had population densities in excess of seventy-six persons per 100 acres, below the parish level and the county average. Approximately 50 per cent of the townlands on the Leslie estate had population densities of less than fifty persons per 100 acres. These figures probably reflect

Table 19. Population density in the rural townlands in Donagh, 1841

Population density (Persons/100 statute acres)	Townlands in the parish: Number of townlands	Townlands in the parish: % of townlands	Townlands on the Leslie estates: Number of townlands	Townlands on the Leslie estates: % of townlands
91+	16	14	5	9.5
76–90	17	15	4	7.5
61–75	19	16.5	10	19
51–60	19	16.5	8	15
<50	44	8	26	49

Source: *Census of Ireland 1851;* Leslie estate papers rentals (N.L.I., Ms. 5813).

the Leslies' management and administration of their estate, where the tenants were selected and the agents actively monitored how a tenant used the land. The most densely populated rural townland on the Leslie estates was Annaghbeg, with 143 persons per 100 acres, which had been bought as part of the Hutcheson estate in the early nineteenth century. As the holdings on this estate were under an old lease, which Charles Powell Leslie II had tried in vain to buy out, the Leslies would have had less control over how the tenants used the land, compared with the townlands where they had tenants for generations.

The Leslies were never passive during the good and poor years in the economy. Coupled with their active management, the Leslies continued to improve their estates and provide an additional stimulus to the local economy by the presence of their demesne at Glaslough. Coote remarking on Leslies' estate in 1801 referred to it as a place 'where farming is pursued with true spirit, and is rewarded with that success, which a happy love for improvement, and grateful soil will always return.'[96] Wakefield writing later in the early nineteenth century included the Leslies' estate amongst the better ones in the county and is disparaging regarding the estates of Shirley and Bath in comparison, both in the south of the county, which he said exhibited 'the most wretched cultivation . . . and the people complain loudly of middlemen and bad leases'.[97] Gailey's analysis of the buildings in villages referred to earlier also illustrates the Leslies as improving landlords.[98]

The improvements that Charles Powell Leslie II initiated were in a number of forms. Firstly, through improvements to the land on his estate through ditching, reclamation of bogs, etc. Secondly, through the attracting and maintaining skills and agricultural industries, such as mills, to the community through leases. And thirdly, through the introduction of new farming methods and techniques into the community.

Coote describing Leslie's estate at Glaslough in 1801 referred to the reclamation of a 'great tract of bog' to the finest meadow.[99] The correspondence of Leslie's agents illustrates examples of the work which Leslie initiated in the improvement of the lands on his estates. In October 1831, William Murdock described some of the work he was carrying out near Glaslough reporting to Leslie, 'I got the main water course opened from Hillhall and Doagheys to Billis it has done a great deal of good to Billis and Doagheys bogs in a few years it will repay the expense double.'[100] While these were major improvements, he also supported general maintenance improvements to the land on his estates. In August 1815, he paid Hugh Boyland 19*s.* for cleaning thirty-eight perches of drain.[101] In October of the same year, he paid £9. 16*s.* 6*d.* for 'ramparting' in the townland of Astridgemore.[102]

The Leslie estates at Glaslough were known for their woodlands. In the eighteenth century Arthur Young had remarked on the beauty of the woods at Castle Leslie.[103] In 1801, Coote described a hundred-acre ash wood at Glaslough as 'the finest timber in Ireland'.[104] In Wakefield's description of

1812, he wrote 'I passed through the village of Glaslough, belonging to Colonel Leslie, in the environs of which there is abundance of wood.'[105] The estate accounts show that Leslie continued the development of the woodland. In March 1813, Leslie paid £4. 15*s.* 8½*d.* to 'Barney McGonnell and company for planting done in the wood'.[106]

The Leslies' tenants included those who had skills associated with agriculture, which were useful to the local economy. The leases described earlier included one with a blacksmith, John Diven.[107] William Murdock's letter to Leslie in October 1831 identified and recommended a suitable tenant, a miller, for a mill on Leslie's estate at Emy.[108] In fact three of the four mills mentioned in the ordnance survey memoirs on the Leslie estate were built post 1800, in 1809, 1824 and 1836, indicating ongoing development.[109] Additionally, Leslie stimulated trade at Glaslough, which as Coote noted in 1801, shortly after Leslie had inherited the estates, he planned to pay particular attention to.[110] In 1806, Charles Powell Leslie II obtained a patent for a monthly fair at Glaslough.[111]

The Leslies were innovative in the introduction of new farming methods and capabilities into the community. Lewis's account of Donagh in 1837, remarked that 'agriculture is much improved, under the auspices of a farming society which holds its meetings at Glaslough.'[112] At the beginning of the century Coote described 'an excellent enclosed farm-yard' at Glaslough, which 'with the proposed additions' he believed it would be a very complete and large farmyard.[113] In 1810 Charles Powell Leslie II employed Charles Christianson as land steward with the objective of introducing new farming methods and improvements onto Leslie's estates at Glaslough.[114] An Edinburgh doctor named Coventry had recommended Christianson to Leslie describing him 'as an experienced and intelligent man who has himself farmed land and also conducted improvements on some large estates in Scotland . . . being very active and yet cautious, and besides strictly sober and honest'.[115] Christianson's correspondence described his work on Leslie's estates. A letter to Leslie in April 1812 is typical where he wrote, 'Clery is all to be in a state of fallow, the old ditches are now all levelled and we have been and will continue to cut drains in it where wet'.[116] He continued in this letter to describe the layout of the field, which he planted, with different rotations of potatoes, beans, wheat, grass and turnips in different parts of it. However, despite Christianson skills, ability and the work he had done, a dispute arose between him and Leslie and he was sacked in 1812. He appears to have been replaced by John Fleming. The cause of dispute is unclear, however a letter from Alex Henderson to Christianson gives an impression of the force with which Leslie dealt with those who dissatisfied him. Henderson wrote 'the conduct of Col. Leslie is most savage and unjust, there is surely laws in Ireland to give redress to such shocking oppression.'[117]

However, despite the effective and innovative management of their estates by the Leslies, the parish of Donagh and many of the townlands on the Leslie estates suffered significant population drops in the famine years of the 1840s. The parish of Donagh experienced a 33 per cent fall in its rural population between 1841 and 1851.[118] This was higher than the percentage drop for County Monaghan, which was over 29 per cent.[119] Some townlands on the Leslie estates suffered huge population drops. Annaghbeg's population fell from ninety-two in 1841 to thirty-five in 1851, a 60 per cent fall.[120] While other townlands such as Donagh experienced a small drop from 206 in 1841 to 197 in 1851.[121] Throughout the Famine years the Leslies continued to actively manage their estates and assist their tenantry. After the Famine the family led the recovery locally, continuing to develop their estates, building on Charles Powell Leslie II's work, and working with the local community.[122]

The years between 1800 and 1841 were changing times for the community living on the Leslie estates in the parish of Donagh. Initially the community enjoyed the buoyant economic years of the Napoleonic wars. However, the severity of the post-war recession in Donagh and Ireland is obscured by the 1840s famine. The declining incomes in Ireland's rural cottage based linen industry, which many in Donagh were dependent on, exacerbated this recession compounding the post-war decline in living conditions in the parish and changing how people made their living. These changes affected all members of the community, Church of Ireland, Presbyterians and Catholics. Consequently, members of the community migrated from their homes. Some of this relocation took place within the parish. Emyvale's population grew by approximately 30 per cent between 1821 and 1841, while the demesne town of Glaslough's population decreased over the same years. However, there is also evidence to indicate that there was emigration from this parish, initially from the Church of Ireland community but later from all parts of the community.

Conclusion

Charles Powell Leslie II was a practical, hard-nosed businessman who used his talents and political influence to successfully manage his landed estate business through difficult economic times. Between 1800 and 1840 the business grew and the Leslies' total rental income from their estates near Glaslough increased from £2,263 in 1801 to £10,508 in 1840.[1] This 1840s income included the rents from the additional estates bought by Charles Powell Leslie II. However, the Leslies also managed to gradually grow the rental income from their original Glaslough and Emyvale estates from £4,672 in 1813 to £5,780 in 1840 in depressed economic times, when prices were generally falling.[2] This success refutes some traditional views of Irish landlords and the estate system, which endeavoured to show that the morality and economics of the landed estate system pointed in the same direction.[3] Charles Powell Leslie II achieved this success through the active management of his estates seizing opportunities to grow the business and maintaining control of it through his agents to whom he delegated only limited authority with the expectation that they would act as he commanded. He paid particular attention to the costs in his business and did not engage in the extravagances of many of his contemporaries who chose to re-build their country homes even when the economy was depressed. Instead he continued to live in the house built by his ancestors re-investing his earnings into procuring additional estates and developing his business. He was one of the landed class that were 'already sensible and efficient [who] kept their heads above water, [unlike] the extravagant and lackadaisical [who] crashed mightily into ruin' during the post-war economic recession.[4] As a businessman he was uncompromising towards employees who did not perform as he wished, two of his agents and a land steward were sacked. In his dealings with his tenants he ensured that he was prepared so that the law acted for him, however, although on occasions notices to quit were issued, they do not appear to have translated into actual evictions often. His preference was to ensure long term income, thus when required, he appears to have been pragmatic, adjusting his approach to arrears in recognition of the real difficulties which many of his tenants had during depressed economic years.

Charles Powell Leslie II demonstrated many of the business-focused responses of landlords, to the changing economic times after the Napoleonic wars, identified by Kerby Miller.[5] However, unlike Miller's stereotype, Leslie also demonstrated a belief in the tie between landlord and tenant normally associated with eighteenth-century paternalistic minded landlords. This was especially evident in his treatment of some of his Protestant tenants, particularly the militia. Leslie believed that the Protestant ascendancy in church and state was the best guarantee of the future success of his business and his politics reflected this. Throughout his life he promoted and defended the Protestant cause, opposing Catholic relief bills in parliament. He used his political influence to the advantage of his business both directly and indirectly to lever patronage for himself and his friends. Leslie's policy in managing his estates reflected his politics and effected the settlement and development of the community on his estates. He acted as a broker to this community in north Monaghan. By locating the headquarters of the all Protestant Monaghan staff in Glaslough, he increased the population of the Protestant communities and provided security in the neighbourhood. His visible influences included parading uniformed militia demonstrating their loyalty to Britain, the modern development of buildings in Glaslough and the improvements to the land and the farming practiced on his estates. Less obvious was the generally less densely populated townlands on the Leslie estates compared with other townlands in the parish, a consequence of his approach to managing his estates continued after his death by his widow Christina.

This study has shown the impact of the economic crisis from 1815 to 1820 on the estate's community and in particular the severity of the 1817 famine. As Maguire has commented, it was this crisis rather than the famine of the 1840s that 'mark the real watershed between the land situation as it was in the eighteenth century and the crisis of the late nineteenth century.'[6] The emigration movement, which was triggered by the post-war recession, although minor in comparison with the mass movement brought on by the 1840s famine, helped make the later movement possible, by providing help for new emigrants from relatives who had emigrated earlier and by changing how people viewed emigration. Following this post-war crisis many of the community in Donagh chose to emigrate to America. Others relocated within the parish, for example to Emyvale where the population increased significantly.

Fundamentally, the disaster that befell Ireland in the 1840s was too large for individual landlords to address. The social structure and the economy of rural communities like those in Donagh had developed in the eighteenth-century on the momentum of the linen industry boom dependent on the household production unit. Technology and globalisation made this production unit obsolete and changed this industry so that Donagh's household producers were forced to the ends of the production chain. Brenda Collins comments that it was the links to the land structure, which made this household production viable.[7] The unit's options for maintaining a livelihood were originally spread among the varying cash income sources, sale of their flax, hand-spun yarn or woven cloth, and cultivation of their food crop, potatoes. With the industrialisation of spinning, the potato crop, flax growing and weaving, prolonged its existence on decreased revenue margins. The availability of cash income and food crop hid the potential disaster of the failure of either and maintained the inertia of the weaving families despite declining living standards. Collins suggests two ways out of this situation. The first option was a return to peasant farming. However, Monaghan's population density precluded any possibility of the land providing adequate food supply without land reform. The alternative was full waged labour on a non-agrarian basis, which entailed migration.[8] These possibilities support the view that in response to Ireland's post-war economic recession radical changes were needed in the people's thinking, how they earned their living and where they lived, coupled with a massive capital investment to provide them with new livelihoods if the inevitable disaster was to be avoided. But this was beyond the scope, understanding and capacity of the landed gentry, the people themselves and the government administration. Consequently, the disastrous famine of the 1840s steamrolled through an already weakened and vulnerable society. The Leslie estates and the parish of Donagh, like most of Ireland were not to be insulated from this cataclysm.

Today the Leslie family still live at Castle Leslie in Glaslough, maintaining their link with the local community and continuing to adapt to changing times. The current castle was built by Charles Powell Leslie II's son, Sir John Leslie, towards the end of the nineteenth century. The family welcome guests to their home, which they now run as a country-house hotel. Portraits of Charles Powell Leslie II and his wife Christina hang in the dining room. Little evidence of their influence on the development of the community is obvious. However, the attractive villages of Glaslough and Emyvale and the well kept neighbouring farm landscape owe much of their appearance to the activity and efforts of Charles Powell Leslie II and his wife Christina in the early nineteenth century.

Notes

ABBREVIATIONS

C.L.A.	Leslie Estate Papers in the Castle Leslie Archives, Glaslough, County Monaghan
D.P.R.1(a), 1(b), 2 & 3	Donagh parish registers vols. 1(a), 1(b), 2 and 3, Donagh Church of Ireland Archive, Glaslough, County Monaghan.
D.V.B.1	Donagh parish vestries 1731–1818, Donagh Church of Ireland Archive, Glaslough, County Monaghan.
D.V.B.2	Donagh parish vestries 1819–1912, P.R.O.N.I. MIC/1/127/D/2.
H.M.C.	Historical Manuscript Commission
N.A.I.	National Archives of Ireland
N.L.I.	National Library of Ireland
P.R.O.N.I.	Public Record Office of Northern Ireland

Note on Currency: Irish currency was abolished in 1826 and British currency came into use. In this essay monetary values are as in the primary sources except where comparison is made between pre-1826 and post-1826 monetary values, for example rent roll returns. In this latter case, all values have been converted to Irish currency values. The conversion rate of £100 British currency to £108. 6*s*. 8*d*. Irish currency has been used. This was the par conversion rate used during the currency stabilisation period prior to the replacement of Irish currency with British currency. (Source: L.M. Cullen, *An economic history of Ireland since 1660* (2nd edition, London, 1987), p. 107.)

INTRODUCTION

1 K.A. Miller, *Emigrants and exiles* (Oxford, 1985), pp 210, 212–13.
2 W.A. Maguire, *The Downshire estates in Ireland, 1801–1845* (Oxford, 1972), p. 253.
3 J.S. Donnelly jr., *The land and the people of nineteenth century Cork* (London & Boston, 1975), p. 385.
4 Maguire, *Downshire estates*, p. 246.
5 T.W. Freeman, *Pre-famine Ireland* (Manchester, 1957), p. 9.
6 E.P. Shirley, *The history of the county of Monaghan* (London, 1879); Seymour Leslie, *Glaslough in the kingdom of Oriel and noted men who have dwelt there* (Glaslough, 1913).
7 Peadar Livingstone, *The Monaghan story* (Enniskillen, 1980).
8 P.J. Duffy, 'Assisted emigration from the Shirley estate 1843–54' in *Clogher Record*, xiv, (1992), pp 7–62; P.J. Duffy, 'The famine in County Monaghan' in Christine Kinealy, Trevor Parkhill (eds), *The famine in Ulster* (Belfast, 1997), pp 169–95.
9 Martin Cahill, 'The 1826 general election in County Monaghan' in *Clogher Record*, v, (1964), pp 166–7.
10 Brendan O'Grady, 'The Monaghan settlers', in *The Abegweit Review*, (University of Prince Edward Island, Canada), (Spring 1983), pp 63–4.
11 Cahill, '1826 election', pp 161–183; Christopher McGimpsey, 'County Monaghan elections 1800–68', unpublished thesis (P.R.O.N.I., ENVS/HP/23/1 Part 1.) (hereafter cited as McGimpsey, 'Monaghan elections'); A.T.Q. Stewart, *The summer soldiers the 1798 rebellion in Antrim and Down* (Belfast, 1995).
12 Pedigree of Leslie of Glaslough, with descent from Bartholdus of Leslie,

1090–1842, (N.L.I., Ms. 174); Pedigree of Leslie of Castle Leslie, Glaslough, Co. Monaghan, Barts. (N.L.I., Ms. 180); Songs sung and election addresses given in favour of Colonel Charles Powell Leslie and Evelyn J Shirley, at an election in Monaghan, 26 June 1826 (N.L.I., Ms. 1420); Rental of the estate of Robert Leslie Glaslough, Co. Monaghan, 1751–1766 (N.L.I., Ms. 5783); Rental of Glaslough and Emy estates of the Leslie family in Co. Monaghan, 1765–1780 and 1802 (N.L.I., Ms. 5809); Rental of the Monaghan and Tyrone estate of the Leslie family, 1840, 1846 (N.L.I., 5813); Rental of the Glaslough and Emy estate, Co. Monaghan, 1752 & 1768–1779 (N.L.I., Ms. 13,719).

13 Samuel Lewis, *A topographical dictionary of Ireland* (2 vols., London, 1837); Sir Charles Coote, *Statistical survey of the county of Monaghan with observations on the means of improvement* (Dublin, 1801).

THE LESLIES OF GLASLOUGH AND THE PARISH OF DONAGH

1 Leslie, *Glaslough*, p. 14; Shirley, *History of Monaghan*, p. 135.
2 Shirley, *History of Monaghan*, p. 142.
3 Leslie, *Glaslough*, pp 14–15.
4 N.L.I., Ms. 174; N.L.I., Ms. 180.
5 Shirley, *History of Monaghan*, p. 149.
6 Dr Charles Leslie to the duke of Mar, 25 March 1718 (H.M.C., *Stuart Mss.* (7 vols, London, 1902–23), vi, p. 195).
7 James III to Lieutenant-general Dillon, 6 May 1718 (H.M.C., *Stuart Mss.* vi, 1916, pp 406–8).
8 Shirley, *History of Monaghan*, p. 147.
9 Letter to the electors of the County Monaghan, 15 June 1826 (N.L.I., Ms. 1420).
10 N.L.I., Ms. 174; N.L.I., Ms. 180.
11 *Journals of the house of commons of the kingdom of Ireland* (19 vols, Dublin, 1796–1800), iv, p. 168.
12 1736 Sale Book (C.L.A., H1).
13 Leslie, *Glaslough*, p. 20.
14 Arthur Young, *A tour in Ireland 1776–1779*, ed. by A.W. Hutton (2 vols, London, 1892, reprinted Shannon, 1970), i, p. 125.
15 N.L.I., Ms. 13,719.
16 Shirley, *History of Monaghan*, p. 148.
17 N.L.I., Ms. 13,719.
18 Rentals of Glaslough and Emy estate, 1800–21 (C.L.A., D1).
19 N.L.I., Ms. 5783.
20 Peter Collins, *County Monaghan sources in the Public Record Office of Northern Ireland* (Belfast, 1998), p. 57.
21 D.C. Rushe, *History of Monaghan for two hundred years 1660–1860*, (Dundalk, 1921), p. 349.
22 R.G. Thorne (ed.), *The history of parliament, the house of commons, 1790–1820* (London, 1986) iv, p. 416; Collins, *County Monaghan sources*, p. 58.
23 Thorne, *History of parliament, 1790–1820*, iv, p. 416.
24 Collins, *County Monaghan sources*, p. 59.
25 N.L.I., Ms. 174; N.L.I., Ms. 180.
26 Thorne, *History of parliament, 1790–1820*, iv, p. 416.
27 Thorne, *History of parliament, 1790–1820*, iv, p. 416.
28 Thorne, *History of parliament, 1790–1820*, iv, p. 416.
29 1796–1816 commissions (C.L.A., J5/1).
30 Thorne, *History of parliament, 1790–1820*, ii, p. 679.
31 Thorne, *History of parliament, 1790–1820*, iv, pp 416–7.
32 B.M. Walker (ed.), *Parliamentary election results in Ireland, 1801–1922* (Dublin, 1978) p. xiv.
33 McGimpsey, 'Monaghan elections', p. 9.
34 McGimpsey, 'Monaghan elections', p. 14.
35 Thorne, *History of parliament, 1790–1820*, iv, p. 416.
36 Angelique Day and Patrick McWilliams (ed.), *Ordnance survey memoirs of Ireland, volume 40, counties of south Ulster, 1834–8* (Belfast & Dublin, 1998), p. 98 (hereafter cited as *OS Memoirs*)
37 P.J. Duffy, *Landscapes of south Ulster* (Belfast, 1993), p. 70.
38 Coote, *Statistical survey of Monaghan* p. 159.
39 Date stone on the south side of the church reads '1670 and ReBuilt in 1763'; Shirley, *History of Monaghan* p. 294.
40 Shirley, *History of Monaghan*, pp 553–4.
41 Shirley, *History of Monaghan*, pp 553–4.
42 The Presbyterian historical society of Ireland, *A history of the Presbyterian*

Church in Ireland 1610–1982 (Belfast, 1982), p. 506.
43 Edward Wakefield, *An account of Ireland statistical and political* (2 vols. London, 1812), ii, p. 307.
44 Wakefield, *Account of Ireland*, ii, p. 620.
45 D.P.R.1(a).
46 D.V.B.1, pp 300, 323, 337.
47 D.V.B.2, f. 3.
48 P.R.O.N.I., MIC/1P/155/1, Glennan Presbyterian marriages, 1805–20.
49 Coote, *Statistical survey of Monaghan*, pp 150, 156.
50 Coote, *Statistical survey of Monaghan*, pp 30, 150.
51 Coote, *Statistical survey of Monaghan*, pp 152–4.
52 Lewis, *Dictionary of Ireland*, i, p. 465.
53 Coote, *Statistical survey of Monaghan*, p. 156.
54 *OS Memoirs*, p. 101.
55 Lewis, *Dictionary of Ireland*, i, p. 464.
56 *OS Memoirs*, p. 101.
57 *OS Memoirs*, p. 101.
58 *OS Memoirs*, p. 101.
59 Lewis, *Dictionary of Ireland*, i, p. 657.
60 Lewis, *Dictionary of Ireland*, i, p. 465.
61 Letters related to the lease between Charles Powell Leslie and William Ogle (C.L.A., J1/1).
62 N.L.I., Ms. 5809; N.L.I., Ms. 13,719; N.L.I., Ms. 5783.
63 Survey of plantation acres, tenants, houses, mills, etc. on the Glaslough and Emy estates, 1763 (C.L.A., G1/3).
64 Coote, *Statistical survey of Monaghan*, p. 155.
65 *Abstract of answers and returns under the population Acts 55 Geo.III, enumeration 1821*, pp 306–7, H.C. 1824 (577) xxii (hereafter cited as Census of Ireland 1821).
66 *Abstract of answers and returns under the population Acts 55 Geo.III, 3 Geo.IV, 2 Geo.IV,* 1. *Will.IV, enumeration 1831*, pp 276–7, H.C. 1833 (634), xxxix (hereafter cited as *Census of Ireland 1831*); *Report of the commissioners appointed to take the census of Ireland for the year 1841*, pp 344–5, H.C. 1843 (504), xxiv (hereafter cited as *Census of Ireland* 1841).
67 *OS Memoirs*, p. 99.
68 Coote, *Statistical survey of Monaghan*, p. 154.
69 *OS Memoirs*, p. 99.
70 Alan Gailey, *Rural houses of the north of Ireland* (Edinburgh, 1984), p. 94.
71 *OS Memoirs*, p. 100.
72 *Second report of public instruction, Ireland*, p. 22a-3a, H.C. 1835, xxxiv.
73 *Census of Ireland 1821*, pp 306–7; *Census of Ireland 1831*, pp 276–7; *Census of Ireland 1841*, pp 344–5.
74 *First report from his majesty's commissioners for inquiring into the condition of the poorer classes in Ireland, appendix (D) supplement [36]*, p. 378, H.C. 1836, xxxi (hereafter cited as *Poor inquiry*); *Poor inquiry, appendix (F) supplement [38]*, p. 378, H.C. 1836, xxxiii.
75 *Census of Ireland 1841*, pp 344–5.
76 *Census of Ireland 1841*, p. 348.
77 Liam Kennedy, 'The rural economy. 1820–1914' in Liam Kennedy, Philip Ollerenshaw (eds), *An economic history of Ulster, 1820–1940* (Manchester, 1985), pp 4–5.
78 Brenda Collins, 'Proto-industrialisation and pre-famine emigration' in *Social History*, vii, (1982), pp 140–1.
79 *Report of the commissioners appointed to inquire into the state of the fairs and markets in Ireland*, p. 102, H.C. 1852–3 (1674), xli (hereafter cited as *Fairs and markets*).
80 Lewis, *Dictionary of Ireland*, i, p. 657.
81 Coote, *Statistical survey of Monaghan*, p. 226.
82 William Carleton, 'The fair of Emyvale' in *The Northern Standard*, 1 August 1906.
83 Carleton, 'Fair of Emyvale'.
84 Leslie, *Glaslough*, facing p. 50.
85 Charles Gavan Duffy, *My life in two hemispheres* (2 vols London, 1898, reprinted Shannon, 1968), i, p. 13.
86 P. O'Snodaigh, 'Notes on the volunteers, militia, yeomanry and orangemen of County Monaghan' in *Clogher Record*, ix, (1977), p. 163.
87 Sir Richard Musgrave, *Memoirs of the Irish rebellion of 1798* (4th ed., Indiana, 1995), p. 149.
88 Livingstone, *Monaghan story*, p. 171.
89 P.R.O.N.I., MIC/1P/155/1, Glennan Presbyterian marriages.
90 P.R.O.N.I., MIC/1P/155/1, Glennan Presbyterian marriages.

91 Manuscript copy of William Watson's, 'Some records of the Monaghan regiment of militia from its being raised in the year 1793 to the present period 1870, Monaghan, 1870' (C.L.A., J 6/10, f. 14). (hereafter cited as, Monaghan militia).
92 Monaghan militia, f. 14.
93 Letter from Dublin Castle to Leslie, 9 December 1817 (C.L.A., J5/2).

THE BUSINESS OF MANAGING A LANDED ESTATE

1 Wills and settlements (C.L.A., C5).
2 C.L.A., D1.
3 C.L.A., D1.
4 Tithe applotment book, Donagh parish, County Monaghan, p. 3. (N.A.I., T.A.B. 23/2)
5 C.L.A., D1.
6 A map of the Hutcheson estate in the county of Monaghan and barony of Trough, surveyed by Henry Neil in July 1788 (C.L.A., G1/10); C.L.A., D1.
7 C.L.A., D1.
8 Glaslough and Emyvale rental 1821–1839 (C.L.A., D1A)
9 C.L.A., D1; C.L.A., D1A.
10 James Nixon to Charles Powell Leslie, 3 July 1822 (C.L.A., J3/2).
11 Letters related to the John Rawdon court case, (C.L.A., J2/1); L.M. Cullen, *An economic history of Ireland since 1660* (2nd ed. London, 1987), p. 102.
12 C.L.A., D1A.
13 C.L.A., D1A.
14 C.L.A., J2/1.
15 C.L.A., D1.
16 C.L.A., D1.
17 C.L.A., D1.
18 C.L.A., J2/1.
19 1742, 1763–1841, 1873 box of leases of premises in Glaslough, (C.L.A., B2).
20 C.L.A., J2/1.
21 Robert Murdock to Charles Powell Leslie, 3 December 1817 (C.L.A., J2/8).
22 Robert Murdock to Charles Powell Leslie, 26 January 1819 (C.L.A., J2/8).
23 C.L.A., D1.
24 C.L.A., D1A.
25 D.V.B.1, p. 323; D.V.B.2, p. 8.
26 C.L.A., D1A.
27 William Murdock to Charles Powell Leslie, 21 March 1818 (C.L.A., J2/8).
28 William Murdock to Charles Powell Leslie, 20 October 1831 (C.L.A., J2/8).
29 D.V.B.$_2$, p. 8; Songs sung, and election addresses given in favour of Colonel Charles Powell Leslie and Evelyn J. Shirley, at an election in Monaghan, June 26, 1826 (N.L.I., Ms. 1420); *OS Memoirs*, p. 103.
30 C.L.A., D1A.
31 Pettigo estate correspondence (C.L.A., J2/2).
32 List of militia and fencible officers 1798 (C.L.A., J5/2).
33 Monaghan militia, ff 12, 14.
34 1816–23 rentals of Cordoo/Corduff (C.L.A., D4).
35 James Nixon to Charles Powell Leslie, 21 April 1815 (C.L.A., J3/1).
36 James Nixon to Charles Powell Leslie, 9 June 1824 (C.L.A., J3/1).
37 James Nixon to Charles Powell Leslie, 12 July 1823 (C.L.A., J3/2).
38 James Nixon to Charles Powell Leslie, 25 April 1824 (C.L.A., J3/3).
39 James Nixon to Charles Powell Leslie, 19 April 1831 (C.L.A., J3/3).
40 James Nixon to Charles Powell Leslie, 14 June 1831 (C.L.A., J3/3).
41 James Nixon to Charles Powell Leslie, 6 July 1831 (C.L.A., J3/3).
42 James Nixon to Charles Powell Leslie, 14 June 1822 (C.L.A., J3/2).
43 James Nixon to Charles Powell Leslie, 19 January 1824 (C.L.A., J3/3).
44 N.L.I., Ms. 1420.
45 Monaghan militia, f. 13.
46 D.P.R.$_2$, p. 28.
47 D.P.R.$_2$, p. 18.
48 D.P.R.$_2$, pp 35, 41.
49 Rentals 1821–31 Lower Trough and Garvey estates with purchase value of 1821 (C.L.A., D5).
50 N.L.I., Ms. 1420.
51 D.P.R.1(b), p. 3.
52 C.L.A., C 5.
53 Letters, accounts and receipts to Charles Powell Leslie from Blayney Owen Mitchell (C.L.A., J2/3).
54 Collins, *County Monaghan sources*, p. 73.
55 N.L.I., Ms. 13,719.
56 N.L.I., Ms. 13,719; N.L.I., Ms. 5809; N.L.I., Ms. 5783.

57 C.L.A., D1.
58 Lease between John Diven and Charles Powell Leslie, 10 September 1810 (C.L.A., B2).
59 1805 instructions for leases on the County Donegal estate (C.L.A., B1).
60 Lease between Richard Benson and Charles Powell Leslie's trustees, 16 December 1834 (C.L.A., B1).
61 William Murdock to Charles Powell Leslie, 21 March 1818 (C.L.A., J2/8).
62 List of types of lease on the Glaslough and Emyvale estate c.1789–1810 (C.L.A., B2). This document is undated, however one of the leases listed commenced in 1789 for 21 years, thus giving the approximate date.
63 C.L.A., D1.
64 C.L.A., D1A.
65 Lease between John Diven and Charles Powell Leslie, 10 September 1810 (C.L.A., B2).
66 Lease between Richard Benson and Charles Powell Leslie's trustees, 16 December 1834 (C.L.A., B1).
67 Lease between William Crookshanks and Patrick Boyland, 13 June 1795 (C.L.A., B1).
68 D.V.B.1, pp 293–4.
69 D.V.B.1, p. 298.
70 1798–1819 Vouchers, (C.L.A., E3).
71 C.L.A., E3.
72 T. Mosley to Charles Powell Leslie, 20 September 1812, (C.L.A., J2/7).
73 C.L.A., E3.
74 James Nixon to Charles Powell Leslie, 21 April 1815 (C.L.A., J3/1).
75 Maguire, *Downshire estates*, p. 19.
76 *Evidence taken before her majesty's commissioners of inquiry into the state of the law and practice in respect to the occupation of land in Ireland, part 1*, pp 840–1, 875–6, H.C. 1845 (606), xix.
77 Monaghan militia, ff 12–14.
78 C.L.A., D1.
79 Monaghan militia, f. 15.
80 Monaghan militia, f. 15.
81 James Nixon to Charles Powell Leslie, 21 April 1815 (C.L.A., J3/1).
82 A.P.W. Malcolmson, *Eighteenth century Irish official papers in Great Britain* (2 vols. Belfast, 1990), ii, p. 145.
83 Leslie to Wellesley, 21 May 1807 (P.R.O.N.I., T.2627/3/2: 127); Thorne (ed.), *History of parliament, 1790–1820*, iv, p. 416.
84 Thorne, *History of parliament, 1790–1820*, iv, p. 417.
85 Landed proprietors of Monaghan to Charles Powell Leslie, 29 June 1826 (N.L.I. Ms.1420).
86 Charles Powell Leslie to the landed proprietors of Monaghan, 6 July 1826 (N.L.I. Ms.1420).
87 Charles Powell Leslie to friends, 14 December 1826 (N.L.I. Ms.1420).

THE ESTATE AND ITS COMMUNITY IN CHANGING TIMES

1 Collins, 'Proto-industrialisation', p. 135.
2 Connell, *Population of Ireland*, pp 1–3.
3 Brendan O'Grady, 'A people set apart: the County Monaghan settlers in Prince Edward Island' in *Clogher Record*, xii, (1985), p. 23.
4 W. S. Mason, *Statistical account of Ireland* (3 vols, Dublin, 1814–19) iii, p. xliv; *Census of Ireland 1821*, pp 306–7.
5 K. H. Connell, *The population of Ireland*, (Oxford, 1950) pp 52, 57–9, 79, 82.
6 Miller, *Emigrants*, pp 194, 196–9, 227.
7 P.R.O.N.I., MIC/1P/155/1, Glennan presbyterian marriages, 1805–20.
8 *First report of the commissioners of public instruction, Ireland*, pp 12a-13a, H.C. 1835, xxxiii (hereafter cited as *First report public instruction*).
9 Miller, *Emigrants*, p. 228.
10 C.L.A., D1.
11 James Nixon to Charles Powell Leslie, 14 November 1823 (C.L.A., J3/2).
12 C.L.A., D1.
13 C.L.A., D1.
14 C.L.A., D1.
15 James Nixon to Charles Powell Leslie, 16 June 1817 (C.L.A., J3/1).
16 C.L.A., D1.
17 C.L.A., D1.
18 James Nixon to Charles Powell Leslie, 14 June 1831 (C.L.A., J3/3).
19 James Nixon to Charles Powell Leslie, 31 March 1831 (C.L.A., J3/3).
20 C.L.A., D1.
21 N.L.I., Ms. 5813.
22 N.L.I., Ms. 5813.
23 N.L.I., Ms. 5813.

24 Maguire, *Downshire estates*, pp 52–62.
25 Maguire, *Downshire estates*, p. 61.
26 C.L.A., D1.
27 C.L.A., D1.
28 C.L.A., J2/3.
29 Notice to quit, 21 April 1810 (C.L.A., B1).
30 C.L.A., D1; C.L.A., D1A.
31 James Nixon to Charles Powell Leslie, 6 October 1823 (C.L.A., J3/2).
32 Robert Murdock to Charles Powell Leslie, 4 May 1819 (C.L.A., J2/8).
33 Undated leasebook c.1840 (C.L.A., B1).
34 D.V.B.$_1$, p. 349.
35 D.V.B.$_1$, p. 353.
36 D.V.B.$_1$, p. 354.
37 D.V.B.$_1$, p. 356.
38 P.R.O.N.I., MIC/1P/155/1, Glennan Presbyterian baptisms, 1805–41.
39 C.L.A., D1.
40 D.P.R.1(a), 1(b), 2 & 3.
41 Connell, *Population of Ireland*, p. 230.
42 Livingstone, *Monaghan Story*, p. 177.
43 D.P.R.2.
44 Connell, *Population of Ireland*, p. 232.
45 *OS Memoirs*, p. 104.
46 Captain Ross to Mrs Leslie, 4 July 1831 (C.L.A., D5).
47 James Nixon to Charles Powell Leslie, 19 April 1831 (C.L.A., J3/3).
48 Kennedy, 'Rural economy', p. 32.
49 *Poor inquiry, appendix (E)*, p. 378.
50 *Poor inquiry, appendix (E)*, p. 378.
51 *Poor inquiry, appendix (E)*, p. 378.
52 *Poor inquiry, appendix (E)*, p. 378.
53 *Poor inquiry, appendix (B)*, p. 239.
54 *Poor inquiry, appendix (D)*, p. 378.
55 *Poor inquiry, appendix (D)*, p. 378.
56 *Poor inquiry, appendix (D)*, p. 378.
57 *Poor inquiry, appendix (D)*, p. 378.
58 *Poor inquiry, appendix (D)*, p. 378.
59 *Poor inquiry, appendix (D)*, p. 378.
60 *Poor inquiry, appendix (F)*, p. 378.
61 *Poor inquiry, appendix (F)*, p. 378.
62 *Poor inquiry, appendix (F)*, p. 378.
63 *Poor inquiry, appendix (D)*, p. 378.
64 *Poor inquiry, appendix (B)*, p. 239.
65 *Poor inquiry, appendix (B)*, p. 129.
66 *OS Memoirs*, p. 103.
67 *OS Memoirs*, p. 105.
68 *OS Memoirs*, p. 105.
69 *OS Memoirs*, p. 105.
70 *OS Memoirs*, p. 103.
71 *OS Memoirs*, pp 103–5.
72 *OS Memoirs*, p. 104.
73 *Poor inquiry, appendix (E)*, p. 378.
74 *Poor inquiry, appendix (D)*, p. 378.
75 *Poor inquiry, appendix (E)*, p. 378.
76 Robert Murdock to Charles Powell Leslie II, 20 October 1831 (C.L.A., J2/8).
77 *Poor inquiry, appendix (E)*, p. 378.
78 Connell, *Population of Ireland*, p. 28.
79 *Poor inquiry, appendix (F)*, p. 378.
80 *Poor inquiry, appendix (F)*, p. 378.
81 D.P.R.3, p. 53.
82 *Poor inquiry, appendix (F)*, p. 378.
83 *Poor inquiry, appendix (F)*, pp. 377–8.
84 O'Grady, 'Monaghan settlers', pp 63–4.
85 Miller, *Emigrants*, p. 216.
86 The Irish plantation acre has been taken as equivalent to 1.62 statute acres.
87 *Poor inquiry, appendix (F)*, p. 378.
88 *Poor inquiry, appendix (F)*, p. 378.
89 *Poor inquiry, appendix (F)*, p. 378.
90 Maguire, *Downshire estates*, p. 38.
91 *Census of Ireland 1831*, pp 276–7.
92 Freeman, *Pre-famine Ireland*, p. 18.
93 Duffy, 'The famine in Monaghan', p. 171.
94 Duffy, 'The famine in Monaghan', p. 171.
95 Duffy, 'The famine in Monaghan', p. 171.
96 Coote, *Statistical survey of Monaghan*, p. 154.
97 Wakefield, *An account of Ireland*, i, p. 269.
98 Gailey, *Rural houses*, p. 94.
99 Coote, *Statistical survey of Monaghan*, p. 154.
100 William Murdock to Charles Powell Leslie, 20 October 1831 (C.L.A., J2/8).
101 C.L.A., D1.
102 C.L.A., D1.
103 Young, *Tour in Ireland*, i, p. 125.
104 Coote, *Statistical survey of Monaghan*, p. 30.
105 Wakefield, *Account of Ireland*, i, p. 269.
106 C.L.A., E3.
107 Lease between John Diven and Charles Powell Leslie, 10 September 1810 (C.L.A., B2).
108 William Murdock to Charles Powell Leslie, 20 October 1831 (C.L.A., J2/8).
109 *OS Memoirs*, p. 101.

110 Coote, *Statistical survey of Monaghan*, p. 154.
111 *Fairs and markets*, p. 102; Lewis, *Dictionary of Ireland*, i, p. 657.
112 Lewis, *Dictionary of Ireland*, i, p. 464.
113 Coote, *Statistical survey of Monaghan*, p. 154.
114 Christianson to Charles Powell Leslie, 10 November 1810 (C.L.A., J2/7).
115 Coventry to Charles Powell Leslie, 2 October 1810 (C.L.A., J2/7).
116 Christianson to Charles Powell Leslie, 19 April 1812 (C.L.A., J2/7).
117 Henderson to Christianson, 10 October 1812 (C.L.A., J2/7).
118 *The census of Ireland for the year 1851 pt. 1, vol. III, province of Ulster*, p. 283, H.C. 1852–53 (1575), xcii (hereafter cited as *Census of Ireland 1851, pt. 1, vol. III, Ulster*).
119 Duffy, 'The famine in Monaghan', p. 185.
120 *Census of Ireland 1851, pt. 1, vol. III, Ulster*, p. 281.
121 *Census of Ireland 1851, pt. 1, vol. III, Ulster*, p. 282.
122 Collins, *County Monaghan sources*, pp 59–61.

CONCLUSION

1 C.L.A., D1; C.L.A., D1A; N.L.I., Ms. 5813.
2 C.L.A., D1; C.L.A., D1A; N.L.I., Ms. 5813.
3 Cormac Ó Gráda 'Poverty, population, and agriculture, 1801–45' in W.E. Vaughan (ed.), *A new history of Ireland, volume v, Ireland under the union, i, 1801–70* (Oxford, 1989), p. 128.
4 K.T. Hoppen, *Elections, politics, and society in Ireland 1832–1885* (Oxford, 1984), p. 112.
5 Miller, *Emigrants*, pp 210, 212–3.
6 Maguire, *Downshire estates*, p. 250.
7 Collins, 'Proto-industrialisation', p. 142.
8 Collins, 'Proto-industrialisation', p. 142.

Maynooth Research Guides for Irish Local History

IN THIS SERIES

1 Raymond Refaussé, *Church of Ireland Records*
2 Terry Dooley, *Sources for the History of Landed estates in Ireland*
3 Patrick J. Corish and David Sheehy, *Records of the Irish Catholic Church*
4 Jacinta Prunty, *Maps and Mapmaking in Local History*

Maynooth Studies in Irish Local History

IN THIS SERIES

1 Paul Connell, *Parson, Priest and Master: National Education in Co. Meath 1824–41*
2 Denis A. Cronin, *A Galway Gentleman in the Age of Improvement: Robert French of Monivea, 1716–79*
3 Brian Ó Dálaigh, *Ennis in the 18th Century: Portrait of an Urban Community*
4 Séamas Ó Maitiú, *The Humours of Donnybrook: Dublin's Famous Fair and its Suppression*
5 David Broderick, *An Early Toll-Road: The Dublin–Dunleer Turnpike, 1731–1855*
6 John Crawford, *St Catherine's Parish, Dublin 1840–1900: Portrait of a Church of Ireland Community*
7 William Gacquin, *Roscommon Before the Famine: The Parishes of Kiltoom and Cam, 1749–1845*
8 Francis Kelly, *Window on a Catholic Parish: St Mary's Granard, Co. Longford, 1933–68*
9 Charles V. Smith, *Dalkey: Society and Economy in a Small Medieval Irish Town*
10 Desmond J. O'Dowd, *Changing Times: Religion and Society in Nineteenth-Century Celbridge*
11 Proinnsíos Ó Duigneáin, *The Priest and the Protestant Woman*
12 Thomas King, *Carlow: the manor and town, 1674–1721*
13 Joseph Byrne, *War and Peace: The Survival of the Talbots of Malahide 1641–1671*
14 Bob Cullen, *Thomas L. Synnott: The Career of a Dublin Catholic 1830–70*
15 Helen Sheil, *Falling into Wretchedness: Ferbane in the late 1830s*
16 Jim Gilligan, *Graziers and Grasslands: Portrait of a Rural Meath Community 1854–1914*
17 Miriam Lambe, *A Tipperary Estate: Castle Otway, Templederry 1750–1853*
18 Liam Clare, *Victorian Bray: A Town Adapts to Changing Times*

Maynooth Studies in Irish Local History (cont.)

19 Ned McHugh, *Drogheda before the Famine: Urban Poverty in the Shadow of Privilege 1826–45*

20 Toby Barnard, *The Abduction of a Limerick Heiress: Social and political relations in mid eighteenth-century Ireland*

21 Seamus O'Brien, *Famine and Community in Mullingar Poor Law Union, 1845–1849: Mud Huts and Fat Bullocks*

22 Séamus Fitzgerald, *Mackerel and the Making of Baltimore, Co. Cork, 1879–1913*

23 Íde Ní Liatháin, *The Life and Career of P.A. McHugh, 1859–1909: A Footsoldier of the Party*

24 Miriam Moffitt, *The Church of Ireland Community of Killala and Achonry 1870–1940*

25 Ann Murtagh, *Portrait of a Westmeath Tenant Community, 1879–85: The Barbavilla Murder*

26 Jim Lenehan, *Politics and Society in Athlone, 1830–1885: A Rotten Borough*

27 Anne Coleman, *Riotous Roscommon: Social Unrest in the 1840s*

28 Maighréad Ní Mhurchadha, *The Customs and Excise service in Fingal, 1684–1765: Sober, Active and Bred to the Sea*

29 Chris Lawlor, *Canon Frederick Donovan's Dunlavin 1884–1896: A west Wicklow village in the late nineteenth century*

30 Eithne Massey, *Prior Roger Outlaw of Kilmainham*

31 Terence A.M. Dooley, *The Plight of the Monaghan Protestants, 1912–26*

32 Patricia Friel, *Frederick Trench, 1746–1836 and Heywood, Queen's County the creation of a romantic landscape*

33 Tom Hunt, *Portlaw, county Waterford 1825–76, Portrait of an industrial village and its cotton industry.*

34 Brian Gurrin, *A century of struggle in Delgany and Kilcoole: An exploration of the social implications of population change in north-east Wicklow, 1666–1779*

35 William H. Crawford, *The Management of a Major Ulster Estate in the Late Eighteenth Century. The Eighth Earl of Abercorn and his Irish Agents*

36 Maeve Mulryan Moloney, *Nineteenth-century elementary education in the archdiocese of Tuam*

37 Fintan Lane, *In Search of Thomas Sheahan: Radical Politics in Cork, 1824–1836*

38 Anthony Doyle, *Charles Powell Leslie (II)'s estates at Glaslough, County Monaghan, 1800–41: Portrait of a landed estate business and its community in changing times*

39 Mealla C. Ní Ghiobúin, *Dugort, Achill Island, 1831–1861: A study of the rise and fall of a missionary community*

40 Frank Cullen, *Cleansing rural Dublin: public health and housing initiatives in the South Dublin poor law union 1880–1920*